Miracles
TODAY

Miracles TODAY

True Stories of Contemporary Healings

HENRY LIBERSAT

CHARIS

SERVANT PUBLICATIONS
ANN ARBOR, MICHIGAN

Charis Books is an imprint of Servant Publications especially designed to serve
Roman Catholics.

Published by Servant Publications
P.O. Box 8617
Ann Arbor, Michigan 48107

Cover design: Eric Walljasper

99 00 01 02 10 9 8 7 6 5 4 3 2 1

Printed in the United States of America
ISBN 1-56955-107-3

LIBRARY OF CONGRESS CATALOGING-IN-PUBLICATION DATA

Libersat, Henry.
    Miracles today : true stories of contemporary miracles / reported by Henry
Libersat.
        p.   cm
    ISBN 1-56955-107-3 (alk. paper)
    1. Spiritual healing Case studies.   2. Christian life—Catholic authors.   I.
Title.
BT732.55.L53   1999
234'.131—dc21   99-33944
                                                       CIP

TO

Bishop Sam Jacobs
who knows and teaches
the healing power of God,

and

Sister Briege McKenna, O.S.C.,
and **Father Kevin Scallon, C.M.,**
who minister to the
Lord's priests and people,

and

John and Betty Ligas,
dear friends
who work so tirelessly
for Jesus the Lord.

CONTENTS

SPECIAL THANKS

As always, Peggy, my wife, has been so supportive of this work and of all my ministry in the Catholic Church. Peg gave the manuscript a critical read, found errors I had missed and suggested ways in which the material could be smoothed out. She deserves a lot of the credit that people lay at my doorstep.

Editors hate to be edited, but Bert Ghezzi of Servant Publications, who suggested this book, became a gentle, affirming editor and taskmaster. I owe him one (and he'll get it!).

Finally, to all those wonderful people who so willingly spent time with me in interviews by phone or in person, and to those who so graciously granted permission for reprinting material, sincere and heartfelt gratitude.

FOREWORD

God answers prayers. He really does. Sometimes he says no. Sometimes the answer is simply silence. But God answers every prayer we utter. He even hears us before we utter a word. He knows us. He loves us. He knows what is best for us.

Sometimes God lets us go through our own little hells. Sometimes we may have created these hells for ourselves. Often, trials come to us through no fault of our own. God lets us go through these times. He may not send us the answer to prayer that we want but he knows what can come of the situation or suffering. He knows that if we rely on him we will emerge victorious, in one way or another.

In *Miracles Do Happen* (Servant Publications), Sister Briege McKenna, O.S.C., provides Christians with a beautiful and trustworthy exposition of faith, the power of prayer and God's action in our lives. She explains how God is really saying "Yes!" to us even when it seems the answer is "No!" It was my honor, privilege and pleasure to work with her on that book.

This book, *Miracles Today*, is of the same genre but it is not the story of any one person's life and ministry. This book tells the stories of many people who felt God's healing touch. The stories are not organized into a Christian theology on healing but all have a common thread: Ordinary, real life people who, in differing ways, experienced the healing touch and power of God.

As far as possible, though without medical proof in many cases, the stories have been authenticated through the testimony of people who have witnessed the healings claimed in these pages.

The people sharing their stories here have joyously received a "yes" from God. The "yes" of God, as we will see, may have come only slowly, after much pain, frustration or darkness of spirit. The "yes" comes frequently through both prayer and medical treatment. But without exception, even among those who find their own healing due to both medicine and prayer, these people believe God has given them the healing.

The stories testify that God still works miracles today, that he wants to show his love for us through his ever-present power to heal, to deliver, to lift up and to liberate.

ONE

From Pyromania to Paradise

+————◆————+

The late August breeze was cool as it breathed across the grounds of All Hallows Seminary and College in Dublin, Ireland. It was a beautiful afternoon, quiet time in the Intercession for Priests, a retreat held every August.

I had heard about Benny Blumensaat, a man who had a tremendous story of how God had healed him after a long time of suffering and darkness of spirit. I arranged for an interview during the Intercession. I had no idea what a wonderful story I was about to hear.

Benny Blumensaat is the middle child of seven and a native of Aarhus, Denmark. His family is Catholic although the Denmark of Benny's childhood was strongly Lutheran and just as strongly anti-Catholic. Even today, there are only thirty-five thousand Catholics in Denmark.

Benny remembers his father as a hard-working, loving man. Benny can still see his father waving as he and his siblings left for school each morning. One morning, the kids left for school at 7:30. At 10:30, they were called to the school office to learn that their father had died of a blood clot in his heart. Benny was only twelve.

His father's death affected the young Benny deeply and adversely. When he reached thirteen, his life began to change. He had always been a good child who had gone to Mass and been an altar boy. But he was headed for trouble. Benny experienced deep hurt over his father's death but he kept it inside. He was an introvert who just couldn't share his pain. Instead, he lived with it and blamed himself: "What did I do wrong to make my father die?"

With his mother's permission, Benny left school at fifteen and took a job as a gardener. He became involved with a football team and one day, after a game, he and the other players shared a few beers. "I had more than a few," he remembers. He got drunk.

Not long after that he got drunk again. He discovered that when he was drunk he didn't feel the pain. "That began ten years of drinking. When I was drunk, I felt free. I used alcohol as an escape from reality, from the death of my father."

Benny was arrested for drunkenness and lost his driver's license when he was eighteen. He also got in trouble for stealing liquor and cars. "Everyone told me I should stop drinking—my mother, my brothers and sisters, my friends, the priest I knew as a child—but I didn't want anyone to tell me what to do."

When he was nineteen, Benny was arrested for arson. He set two buildings on fire and was arrested again. By the time he was twenty-four, he had set six buildings on fire. Firefighters found him sleeping near four of the fires, and he actually fell asleep in two of the buildings after they went up in flames. He was barely rescued before his own handiwork killed him.

> ## Temperance
>
> The virtue of temperance disposes us to avoid every kind of excess: the abuse of food, alcohol, tobacco or medicine. Those incur grave guilt who, by drunkenness or a love of speed, endanger their own and others' safety on the road, at sea or in the air.
>
> The use of drugs inflicts very grave damage on human health and life. Their use, except for strictly therapeutic grounds, is a grave offense ... (Catechism of the Catholic Church, Nos. 2290-91).

Several times, he moved from prison to hospitals or clinics back to prison. "I never wanted to hurt anyone," Benny said. "But I couldn't control myself when I got drunk." At one point he even attempted suicide. "I didn't want to die, but I didn't know where to turn.

"I believed in God as a God 'out there,'" Benny said. "Now

and then I said a prayer but there was no response. Nobody listened. God was distant. He didn't play a role in my life."

Benny was diagnosed as a pyromaniac. Since he was mentally ill, he had to finish his prison sentence in the mental ward of a hospital. "It was like I was living in darkness. There was no hope, no direction in my life. I had no remorse. I was very bitter."

Eventually, without his knowledge, he was placed in a psychiatric hospital. He was still a prisoner of the state, serving his time in a locked ward.

Around this time, Benny's mother attended a prayer meeting at the invitation of a nun. At the meeting, his mother and thirty other people, including Father Paul Marx, an Oblate priest, prayed for Benny. "In the middle of prayer, a woman went before the crucifix and said, 'Thank you, Jesus, for we know you are healing Benny.' My mother was stunned. She had seen me that day and knew there were no signs of healing in my life. I wanted everyone to leave me alone in my own world.

"One evening, Mother came with Father Paul, the nun who had asked Mother to go to the prayer meeting, and another lady. Mother didn't think I would see Father Paul because I was having nothing to do with priests. In fact, I didn't want to see or talk to anyone. I said to myself 'What now?' but I did see Father because Mother wanted me to." Benny braced himself, expecting the priest to preach at him and tell him how wrong he was.

"But Father Paul told me of his own crises in life," Benny said, "and how people prayed for him and that Jesus helped him when they laid hands on him in prayer. He spoke to me of the Jesus of the Gospels—Jesus, the man of mercy and love. He spoke of Jesus as though he were really there, really alive and present with us. He spoke of Jesus in a joyful and peaceful way. It felt good just sitting there talking to him. I didn't need my defenses up.

"At the end of our meeting, he said, 'OK if I pray for you?' I said yes but asked him if I had to do anything. He said, 'No, just sit. Remember, Jesus sent his disciples to heal in his Name.' I had no expectations but I felt easy being with Father Paul.

"He placed his hands on my head. My mother had a hand on one shoulder and the nun had a hand on my other shoulder. Father Paul prayed first in Danish and then in a strange language. I realize now he was praying in tongues. As he was praying, I felt a sense of peace inside me. I felt it! For many, many years I had no peace at all. I knew something had happened but I didn't know what."

Father Paul commanded the devil to leave Benny, mentioning all the things by which the young man was afflicted.

When the priest, his mother and the other woman left, Benny went back to his room. "I felt a sense of peace coming upon me. There was a presence in my room that I had never before experienced and have not experienced since. It was a warm, accepting presence. I didn't recognize that it was God, but I knew it had something to do with the priest's prayers.

"That night, I knelt and directed a prayer to Jesus. I hadn't prayed in years. The next morning I woke up filled with peace and joy. I realized that God had heard the prayer of the priest

The God Who Prays for Us

The Spirit, too, helps us in our weakness, for we do not know how to pray as we ought; but the Spirit himself makes intercession for us with groanings that cannot be expressed in speech. He who searches hearts knows what the Spirit means, for the Spirit intercedes for the saints as God himself wills (Rom 8:26-27).

and something was happening to me. It was like Jesus was right there with me."

Benny began sharing his experience with other patients and with people who visited the hospital. He didn't find a sympathetic ear when the psychiatrist learned from others about his visitors, described as "a man, a woman in dark clothes and a crying woman." She and others thought he had become involved in a cult.

"The psychiatrist was angry," Benny said, "and she wouldn't allow the priest to come back to visit me. She thought I was suffering from some sort of religious psychosis. But I knew something good had happened to me."

Benny had never read the Bible before but now he had a deep desire for the Word of God. "I started reading passages about how Jesus healed. I read the Gospel of John and learned that Jesus came to save us, that he loved us and died for us, that he rose from the dead for all of us."

With this new-found faith, Benny felt a deep need to go to confession. "I felt I had to put a name on all the bad things I had done. I hadn't understood what Jesus did for us on the cross. I could indeed have a good life—even with my past—but I had to confess that past. Father Marx was not allowed in the hospital so another priest visited me dressed as a layman. He heard my confession. At that moment, years of burdens on my shoulders dropped away."

Within two weeks, Benny was telling everyone about his healing and what Jesus could do in their lives. The psychiatrist kept saying, "Don't tell anyone!" but that didn't stop Benny. People from outside the prison hospital were coming to pray with him.

He felt free and grateful. He wanted to do something for God in return. "I thought I wanted to be a monk. I had read about St. Francis, and I was deeply affected by his life and spirit. I truly wanted to be like him. But a friend said to me, "Slow down, Benny. You're not St. Francis."

He was sent back to the prison, and the psychiatrist at the hospital suggested that he be kept there a long time. However, the judge ruled merely that he should undergo a year and a half of psychiatric treatment.

"During that time, I continued the healing process and learned that healing can indeed *be* a process. At one point I told the doctors to take me off all the drugs because I was healed. They said, 'Maybe so, but it is better to taper off gradually.' I knew I was healed. I had felt that everyone had always pushed me away. Now Jesus loved me. I wanted to follow him because he had been good to me. I still want to follow him.

"At last I was released. With God's help I overcame addiction to alcohol. It was a real healing.

"When I was released, a nun asked me to join the laity associated with her religious community. I entered with all my heart and began to live my faith. One day, the nun asked me, 'Have you ever thought of becoming a priest?' 'Yes,' I replied, 'but I don't have enough studies.'"

Shortly after, the bishop came around. The bishop, well aware of Benny's past, asked him about his education. "He never mentioned my past. I began studying for the priesthood at Allenhall seminary."

Benny Blumensaat, a former firebug and mental patient, now totally healed, was ordained a priest in 1993. His mother's prayers were answered beyond her expectations.

Addressing priests at the Intercession during that beautiful time of prayer in Ireland, Father Benny said: "The priest came to me. I did not first go to him. Jesus came to me. I did not first go to him. It is a great thing to be a priest. To think that Jesus is really here, every day, on the altar. There can be no greater thing. I want nothing more than to be a priest forever."

The pyromaniac, healed of that emotional, mental affliction, still sets fires. Now, he sets aflame human hearts with the fire of God's love.

God still heals. He is doing miracles today.

TWO

Sometimes Pride Gets in the Way

There aren't too many of his kind around these days. You know, the lanky, long-drink-of-water country boy with a drawl and a wit that sneak up on you. Dick Stone is a veritable curiosity but a wonderful one at that. He has a way of saying things. For example, when he finds the price of an item too high, he doesn't come right out and say so. Rather, he sucks on his bottom lip, looks pensive, glances sympathetically at the salesperson and says, "Why, I didn't know you thought so much of it. I'd never dream of separating you from it."

He's "gone through several churches and some of them as glad to see me go as they were to see me come." He chuckles about that. People who don't feel comfortable with Dick Stone are those who can't take truth from a friend, faith with a grin and problems with a spontaneous prayer.

Dick's oldest and most faithful friend is Nita, his wife of many years. Their five children are all out on their own and they have a "passel of grandchildren."

Dick is an unusual man. An Episcopalian, he was the respected leader of the prayer group at the Catholic cathedral parish in Venice, Florida. He surprised everyone one night when he announced he had become a Catholic. Dick and Nita now live in northern Georgia and have become involved in their parish there.

Dick has two healing stories to tell. The first involves his habit of smoking. He was attending an interdenominational prayer service and people were lining up so that Reverend Eve, a woman with a healing ministry, could pray over them. Dick was in line but couldn't figure out what to pray for because "everything was going real good."

"Well," he says, "I was not aware of God's sense of humor or of how sneaky he is. I decided it was safe enough to pray to kick the smoking habit. I figured nothing would happen. When it was my turn, I told Reverend Eve that I wanted to quit smoking. She asked me to give her my pack of cigarettes, and I did. After all, I had another pack in the car, and I couldn't smoke until I got out of the healing service, so what difference did it make? Let's face it, it sounded good.

"But God was serious about this thing, even if I wasn't, and I found I didn't want a cigarette after that prayer meeting. I've never wanted one since, except on rare special occasions. Never enough to pick one up and smoke it, though.

"For this I give honor and praise to the Lord Jesus, for without him I never could have quit."

And then there was that other healing.

Dick admits to being accident-prone, which is one reason

the Lord "has been so busy healing me." He cut off the end of a finger when he was eighteen months old, lost an eye in an accident and hurt his back on the job pulling and lifting major appliances. He later took a job with mosquito control, "a very important ministry in Florida," because the

> ## The Power of United Prayer
>
> "Again I tell you, if two of you join your voices on earth to pray for anything whatever, it shall be granted you by my Father in heaven. Where two or three are gathered in my name, there am I in their midst" (Mt 18:19-20).

work was lighter most of the time. However, he occasionally had to do some heavy lifting and he injured his back again. He ended up in a back brace which he would have to wear the rest of his life. Several times, tired of the rigid brace, he tried to live without it but couldn't.

Dick and Nita became involved in prayer group ministry. They were on teams who interceded for the sick and needy but Dick never asked for prayer. One evening he was in such pain that Nita urged him to request prayer. Dick said, "No, there are others in worse shape than I am, and I can pray for myself when I get home." Dick and Nita had brought a friend to the meeting who said, "Dick, that's nothing but pride. Go and get prayed for."

As Dick tells the story, "After some grumbling and very poor arguments, I consented. The moment I consented, the pain left me, but I knew I must still be prayed over by my brothers and sisters in Christ. They prayed over me. That was in 1976 and after eight years of wearing that brace I was able to take it off. I have never worn it again."

Dick and Nita say that the pain returned only twice, and each time it left when he agreed to have others in the healing ministry pray for him. "But once," Dick said, "it took me two weeks of pain before I could overcome my pride and ask for prayer. It has now been twenty years with no brace, no pain and no restrictions on my work."

THREE

When a Mother Prays, God Listens!

┼══ · ══┼

Sean Callaghan is a successful personal injury lawyer, a quiet, introspective man. He has red hair and blue eyes and when he speaks, he looks you straight in the eye. He is single and deeply dedicated to helping people, especially his clients when they do not receive their due after personal injury. Sean is one of twelve children of parents well known in Florida business and church circles. His mother, Lee, was one of the first lay leaders of the charismatic renewal in Florida.

Sean was healed twice, though he only remembers the recent healing. Lee remembers both very well. Sean basks in his mother's love as well as in her faith. This is a story of a mother's faith and a son's desire to be healed.

Sean describes himself as a skeptic, one "who does the bare minimum in order to be called a Catholic." He smiles as he says it and looks at his mother who smiles back. There is a knowing twinkle in her eye. Sean has had no "goose bump experiences," as some people call them. There have been no "aha moments." He is like Thomas the apostle who said he would believe when there was proof.

The healing he remembers followed a series of scary events that started in January of 1997 and brought him to a doctor in March. His symptoms began with aggravating back pain soon followed by significant stiffness, numbness and loss of sensation in both legs.

Doctors diagnosed the problem as an intramedullary tumor inside the spinal cord itself. The tumor was located just below the neck, technically at the T3–T4 level. Most advised against surgery because the delicate nature of the procedure could have led to paralysis or death. One neurosurgeon said that even a biopsy of the tumor could cause serious motor skills damage. Some thought surgery might be successful, but they "would not know until they got in there."

One doctor prescribed steroids that would only have masked the pain. Sean didn't even fill the prescription.

The good news was that, due to the shape of the tumor, doctors believed it was benign. They agreed that he should wait to see if the symptoms progressed to the point where the risks of surgery were warranted. Doctors expected the tumor to grow and present serious motor skill problems. The final prescription: "We're sorry. Do nothing and wait."

Sean took an active part in trying to resolve the problem. He consulted other people, including nutritionists. He read books on nutrition and alternative supplements that appeared to successfully fight tumors. He took "various types of products" to see if his "immune system could fight this thing." He didn't want to just sit and wait. And there was prayer. Sean prayed for himself and thought a lot about what he would do with his life in the future.

Lee, for her part, believing firmly in the power of prayer and the goodness of God, had hundreds of people praying. She wanted her son to be healed—and she wanted him to experience God's love in a personal way.

Knowing that the Mass is the most perfect and most powerful prayer, she and Sean attended Mass together on Sundays. "Every Sunday," Lee said, "during the consecration of the bread and wine, I would place my hand on Sean's back where the tumor was located and I would ask God to heal him. After two or three months of this prayer, I could feel heat under my hand. This encouraged me, because often in healing prayer, the sensation of warmth or heat is a sign that healing is taking place. Then, as we would go to Communion, I would notice Sean was wiggling his shoulders and scratching his back. He would later tell me he felt an itching sensation in the location of the tumor."

Lee smiled. "I would remind him: 'Remember when you were a little boy and your boo-boo would itch? I would tell you that it was a sign it was getting well. If it's itching, Sean, it's healing.' I think that was the beginning of healing," Lee said. "I think it was a progressive rather than overnight healing."

In January of 1998, Sean had an MRI. It was his first since the previous July. He said, "I convinced the technicians to give

Persistence in Prayer

"Once there was a judge in a certain city who respected neither God nor man. A widow in that city kept coming to him saying, 'Give me my rights against my opponent.' For a time he refused, but finally he thought, 'I care little for God or man, but this widow is wearing me out. I am going to settle in her favor or she will end by doing me violence.'" The Lord said, "Listen to what the corrupt judge has to say. Will not God then do justice to his chosen who call out to him day and night? Will he delay long over them, do you suppose? I tell you, he will give them swift justice. But when the Son of Man comes, will he find any faith on the earth?" (Lk 18:2-8).

me a copy of the films so I could see them right away instead of having to wait a few days to talk to the neurosurgeon.

"I couldn't see the tumor. Previously, my spinal cord had looked like a python that had swallowed something. It had been swollen with the tumor. Now I couldn't see that. It was gone. They had experienced a little trouble with the machine so I thought maybe it was a bad film. All I could see was a faint, faint glimpse of a change in color where the tumor had been prominent.

"So I was concerned it was a bad film. I went to the neurosurgeon and got the MRI report: The swelling was all gone and there was only a faint trace of where the tumor had been. The MRI diagnosis was that it must have been something else, because tumors don't go away. The neurosurgeon said the same thing: It wasn't a tumor. I guess the official diagnosis is that it wasn't a tumor but something else, although they don't know what. The surgeon told me it probably wouldn't happen again."

Sean is convinced that God had a hand in his healing but he is not convinced a healing miracle took place. All the prayers, all the nutrition, all the faith were part of the healing. He is happy he didn't dwell on the negative but took an active part in trying to beat the tumor. He saw the illness as an opportunity to broaden his perspective and to pray more for himself. "I surely believe that God chose to heal me when medical doctors said I would only get worse and the only help in the future would be radiation or surgery."

Sean is playing tennis again, not quite back to form but almost. His left leg is nearly normal and his right leg, which still has some numbness, seems to be improving.

The other healing in Sean's life was instantaneous and miraculous but Sean was too young to remember.

He wanted to go out into his wading pool but the water was quite cold. Lee told him to wait while she got some hot water to pour into the little pool. She picked up a large pot of boiling water. Florence, the housekeeper, was at her side and Sean held the door open for her. Lee tripped over the threshold and dumped all the water on Sean.

"You could see it. His face, shoulders and chest all turned this horrible purplish red and I screamed out, 'My Jesus, mercy!' Immediately the red disappeared. I said, 'Sean, don't you hurt?' And he said, 'No.' I said, 'Don't you even sting?'

And he said, 'No.' And he ran off and played in the pool. I asked Florence, 'Did you see that?' And she said, 'Yes, I saw it and if I hadn't seen it I wouldn't believe it.' It was amazing. I thanked God for the rest of the day."

When Sean developed the spinal disease twenty-nine years later, Lee thought God "would come up with an instant healing, and he didn't. It wasn't until we stormed heaven with prayer and he took those nutritional aids that we saw results. It took that whole effort to bring about the healing.

"When he was burned, he was a little child who needed an instant healing. Now he is a grown man who needed to learn to walk a bit."

Lee tells a story that leaves Sean amused and still skeptical. She says that after he was so instantly healed of the burns, he actually had the gift of healing. One of his sisters, Annie, suffered severe ant bites on one of her legs. Sean laid hands on her leg and prayed and the bites disappeared. That night, Annie was crying. She said the ant bites still hurt. Lee reminded her that Sean had prayed and they had gone away. "But he only prayed for one leg," Annie cried. So, Lee says, Sean prayed for the other leg and the bites instantly disappeared.

Sean chuckles at the story and says, "Hmmm!" But Lee persists: "Remember Sister Jean Hill? She came to visit once and ended up covered with mosquito bites. She called you because she was itching and couldn't get to sleep. You prayed for her and the bites disappeared immediately!" "Hmmm!" Sean smiled, still the skeptic.

Maybe it's the lawyer in him.

FOUR

"Which Healing Story Do You Want?"

"Which healing story do you want?" she asked. With good reason. Fran Fraleigh-Karpiez, who now has her own healing ministry, has had the good grace of significant healings in her own life.

Born in Norwalk, Connecticut, Fran is the only daughter of a father who was a carpenter and a mother who stayed at home to care for her family. Her only siblings are twin boys younger than she.

Today, Fran is married and has two children, an adopted son, Paul, who is 24, and a daughter, Donna Marie, who is 21.

Paul was adopted when doctors told Fran that she could never have children. When he was two years old, they determined that Fran suffered from lupus, an autoimmune disease.

Around this time, Fran attended a prayer meeting of a local prayer group, even though she didn't know much about the charismatic movement. Eventually, not really knowing what it was all about, she asked for prayer so she might be baptized in the Spirit. Baptism in the Spirit occurs when a person invites the Holy Spirit to activate the graces of baptism and confirmation in his or her life. It is not a sacrament, but more like an actual grace that enables the Christian to develop a closer walk with Jesus and to share the faith more effectively.

Two months after this, Fran became pregnant with Donna Marie. Because of her illness, the doctors advised her to have an abortion. "That was never a consideration for me," she quickly adds. Donna Marie was born on March 17, her brother's birthday.

Fran returned to the prayer group and asked for prayers for her health. After some time, she asked the doctors for new tests. They laughed, but gave her the tests. They didn't laugh for long. The tests showed no signs of lupus. She was healed, and to this day there is no sign of the disease.

This marked the beginning of her active involvement in the charismatic renewal. In 1978, she founded an intercessory prayer group in her own parish.

God does still heal today, but as Fran says, "a healing does not mean your life will be free of problems." In 1981, she was ill again. Her immune system was out of whack. She was arthritic. She developed allergies to the medications and her body stopped producing red blood cells. Her doctor sent her to another hospital and said, "I'll never see her alive again."

She was taken off all medication. It was a real time of crisis, a matter of life and death, and the medical staff didn't have much hope for her recovery. Fran had even prepared her funeral Mass.

Her prayer group started a twenty-four-hour vigil, praying for her healing. The day after the vigil, the doctors ran more tests and were surprised to discover her body was again producing red blood cells. One doctor said, "Somebody up there must love you." They put her on steroids, although she dreaded them. Her recovery was so rapid, the doctors couldn't understand it. "They just threw up their hands," Fran said. "Prayer did it."

But that is not the end of the story. Fran said there was one more healing which she has talked about in many healing services.

It was August 20, 1987. She was at her desk in the Catholic Center of the Bridgeport Diocese where she served as coordinator and administrator of the charismatic renewal.

Suddenly she heard a loud explosion. Something hit her head and she "saw stars." She looked up and there was a big hole in the ceiling. She was covered with debris, so she knew something had hit her.

Carpenters had fired a three-inch nail from an air-powered ram gun. The spike went through a hole in a cinder block, through the ceiling and into her head.

People came running into her office. The vicar general said to her, "Fran, I'm going to anoint you." She thought, "The Last Rites! I'm dying!" Then they took her to the hospital. Tests indicated a depressed skull fracture. Somehow, the nail had not stayed in her skull. They found it on her desk.

There Is No Need to Fear

You shall not fear the terror of
the night
nor the arrow that flies by
day;
Not the pestilence that roams
in darkness
nor the devastating plague at
noon.
Though a thousand fall at
your side,
ten thousand at your right
side,
near you it shall not come.

Psalm 91:5-7

At the hospital, in the emergency room, she was riddled with fear. But a Christian friend kept singing in her ear the words from a song based on Scripture, *"And he will bear you up on eagle's wings ... and hold you in the palm of his hand."*

Doctors put her in neurological intensive care and told nurses and friends to keep her awake to see what would happen.

Over the next twenty-four hours, she had a telephone propped to her ear. Her Christian friends continually read the Psalms to her and Fran was deeply comforted by the words, "You shall not fear the terror of the night ..." (Ps 91).

Fran says that in her time of need, "those words took on a whole new meaning. I felt it was a most powerful message."

In the next day or so, Fran received phone calls from her parents, her brothers and many friends who just wanted to wish her well and say, "I love you." A friend with whom she had been at odds for six months called and said, "I was afraid I wouldn't have the chance to say, 'I'm sorry.'" Fran and her friend were reconciled.

Those expressions of love and concern meant much to Fran. "Why," asks Fran, "do we have to wait for such moments to say those life-giving and important words: 'I love you'?"

Prayers were again at work. "Doctors and nurses could see the hole healing in my head," Fran said. And she was home in four days!

Released from the hospital on Sunday, she remembered she was to be interviewed on radio that following Tuesday. She shared how God had worked in her life and in her healing.

The following October, Fran was invited to lead a healing service, something she had never done before. She was a little nervous about it all, but "I put together a good music ministry" she said, "and we did it." She shared her pain, her fear and her victory in God's power. The experience, she says, "reinforced my own faith" as she saw people at the service being healed. She recalls telling God, in preparing for the service, "I'll show up if you do." And, she says, "he did."

FIVE

Personal Testimony of the Author

As author of this book, I hesitated to use personal stories. However, my immediate family has experienced four significant healings that we attribute to prayer. In three of the stories, one involving my wife, Peggy, and two involving our eldest son, David, medicine also played a part. I have personally witnessed other healings that I mention here.

A Rosary, a Vow and a Miracle

One Sunday afternoon in 1950, my friend Dalton introduced me to his girlfriend's sister, Peg. The minute I saw Peg, I knew I would marry her. Peggy was just over thirteen and I was fifteen. Two years later we were indeed married—and no, it wasn't a shotgun wedding.

Why did we marry so young? We lived in rural Louisiana and there was no skating rink, no internet, no huge shopping malls, no video arcades and TV was not generally available. The choices were to get married, go to the seminary or convent or vegetate.

When we married I had already completed a year in college. I left college and went to work in department stores. Within a few years, we had three children, David, Anthony and Karen, with another on the way.

We had stopped going to church but David's near death, when he was just a year old, brought us back and gave us our first encounter with the healing power of prayer.

David had a virus accompanied by vomiting and diarrhea. He became dehydrated and his kidneys shut down. We rushed him to the hospital where the doctors attempted to re-hydrate him. They had him taped down on a piece of plywood—it reminded me of a cross—while intravenous fluid dripped into his sides and thighs. His little body wouldn't absorb the fluid, however, and his sides and thighs got bigger and bigger. I told the nurses something had to be wrong and asked them to call the doctor. They replied that the doctor was due in for his rounds in late afternoon.

All day David cried, "Mommy" and "Da-Da." He would look at us and beg for water. He wanted us to free him from the board and hold him but we couldn't. All we could do was lean close to him, kiss him and try to comfort him. It was a terrible experience for all three of us.

The doctor did arrive around six that evening and when he

saw David he screamed at the top of his voice, "NURSE!"

They rushed David into the operating room. Later the doctor came out and said, "We're trying to find a vein large enough to introduce medicine that will activate his kidneys, but because he's so dehydrated, we're having trouble. We're doing our best."

Peggy was in tears. I walked away, my hands in my pockets. I was sud-

The Power of Prayer

"For whoever asks, receives; whoever seeks, finds; whoever knocks, is admitted. What father among you will give his son a snake if he asks for a fish, or hand him a scorpion if he asks for an egg? If you, with all your sins, know how to give your children good things, how much more will the heavenly Father give the Holy Spirit to those who ask him" (Lk 11:10-13).

denly aware of the rosary in my pocket, a high school graduation present. I hadn't prayed in a long time, but I took out the rosary and began to pray. After a few minutes, I made a vow: "Mother Mary, if David lives, we will not only return to the church, but I will work for the church full time if that is what God wants."

I had no sooner made this promise when the doctor came out all smiles, saying, "He's fine. Your baby will be all right."

David was to experience another healing later.

Mother Mary and a Kidney Stone

The hospital smells permeated the alcove where I waited with my father-in-law. Peggy was in surgery for a kidney stone. She was also five months pregnant with our fourth child.

The doctor had said surgery could not be delayed, even though it was dangerous for the baby. "If you wait," he told me, "you'll lose both wife and baby." In two months' time, the stone had grown from the size of a pinhead to the size of the end portion of one's little finger.

Prayer sustained us as we made the decision to proceed with the surgery. We had grown close to the parish priests in Peggy's home parish, Our Lady of Lourdes, in Erath, and they had introduced us to the novena to Our Lady of Perpetual Help. We had been praying the novena daily and attending the weekly novena at the church, when the doctor discovered Peggy's kidney stone.

For more than two hours now, Peggy had been in surgery. The head nurse, a very military-type nun whom I quickly, but privately, nicknamed Sarge, kept rushing in and out of the operating room. Each time she double-timed by the alcove, I would ask anxiously, "How is she?"

"Fine," Sarge would mutter and rush past. I sensed something was wrong. I was usually tough in such situations, but this time, deep inside, I was afraid and felt threatened.

At last, the double doors swung open and the surgeon came out. He came up to me, scratching his head, and announced, "She stopped breathing." Then he grabbed me because I grew very faint and fell against the wall.

He almost shouted, "No, No! She's not dead! She's alive. Her diaphragm apparently collapsed as a reaction to some drugs. We're pumping air into her with a hand pump and we've called the fire department for a respirator."

The doctor went back into the operating room. I translated all this to my French-speaking father-in-law, who had huge tears rolling down his cheeks. Then, crying myself, I went down the hall, rosary in hand but unable to pray. I

> ## "She Is Not Dead but Asleep"
>
> A Jewish leader asked Jesus to help his dying daughter. While the man was speaking with Jesus, someone said the young girl had already died.
>
> Jesus heard this, and his response was: "Fear is useless; what is needed is trust and her life will be spared." Once he had arrived at the house, he permitted no one to enter with him except Peter, John, James and the child's parents. While everyone wept and lamented her, he said, "Stop crying for she is not dead but asleep." They laughed at him, being certain she was dead. He took her by the hand and spoke these words: "Get up, child." The breath of life returned to her and she got up immediately.... (Lk 8:49-55)

turned the corner and there was a life-size statue of Our Lady of Lourdes. I looked at the statue and said the only prayer I was able to say, "Mother of God! Our children!"

As I walked back toward the operating room, the doors

burst open and out came a smiling doctor. "She's fine! She'll be OK! She's breathing. I'll tell you one thing, on days like this I wish I were back on the farm, behind a plow, looking at the tail end of a couple of mules!"

He said that Peggy had made medical history, that no one who had ever stopped breathing for such a long time had been revived. I don't know if that's true, but it's what he said.

Because of the breathing problem, the operation couldn't proceed. Two weeks later, Peggy was back in the same hospital and the kidney stone was removed.

The baby? Four months later, Mary was born, the biggest, sassiest and healthiest baby of all our children. She came so fast that when Peggy arrived at the hospital, they carried her in, laid her on the table and "caught Mary on the fly."

We had three more children, Suzanne, Angela and Pierre, and we lost four pregnancies. Today all seven children are married, and Peggy is the proud grandmother of eight boys and thirteen girls. I'm a proud Paw-Paw. And there is a great grandchild on the way!

Prayer Heals Bright's Disease

David was about twelve years old when he came back from school one day with his knees swollen to twice their normal size. I thought he had been injured in gymn class playing football so I called the coach. He assured us, as David had, that he had not been injured.

The next day, the swelling was worse and his face was puffy. Our family doctor immediately suspected Bright's Disease. He explained that this was a kidney disease characterized by a breakdown of the kidney's ability to filter out waste from the blood for elimination through the urinary tract.

A specialist confirmed the diagnosis and placed David in the hospital. I asked one of the doctors how serious David's condition was. He said, "He's as sick as he can get without dying."

David was a smart child and realized his condition must be critical. One day he asked me, in a small but steady voice, "Daddy, am I going to die?" I was lying on the cot in his hospital room, praying. I thought for a moment and then said, "Well, David, we never know when we're going to die. You're sick, but we're praying and the doctors are helping you." Then, with utter conviction, I said, "No, Son, you are not going to die." We were still a long way into the woods, but I knew that David would be all right. I believed that our prayers would be answered.

By that time, I was working for the church as a journalist, and I had many people praying for David. One Saturday afternoon, we found out how wonderful it is to be part of the believing church.

I had been visiting a prison in southwest Louisiana, doing stories on prison reform. The Catholic chaplain was Father Maurice Linnehan, a LaSalette priest. On that Saturday afternoon, Father Linnehan drove two hundred miles from the prison to our hospital. He brought David a relic of St. Dominic Savio, the boy saint who knew and loved God so dearly. But there was more. Father Linnehan said that more than two hundred prisoners had attended Mass and received Communion for David and were continuing to pray for him. That is a moment I will never forget: Prisoners who didn't know us or our son were praying for him because he needed prayer.

David ended up under the care of an internationally famous kidney specialist who thought our son might need a kidney transplant. In the midst of this, we moved to Florida where I began work for *The Florida Catholic* newspaper.

David's doctor in Florida examined him and said there was

Dominic Savio, Boy Saint

Dominic Savio (1842-57) was born a peasant in Riva, Italy. When he was only twelve, he came under the influence of St. John Bosco, a man who had a special love for children. Even at that tender age, Dominic had many spiritual gifts: he seemed to know when people were in need and he had the ability to prophesy.

One legend places Dominic between two friends who had grown angry and were now fighting. He came between the two and held up a crucifix for them to see. At the sight of the crucifix, the boys stopped fighting.

Dominic is credited with a vision that influenced Pope Pius IX to restore a Catholic hierarchy to England.

He was only fifteen when he died. Nearly two hundred years later, Pope Pius XII declared Dominic a saint.

no need for a transplant. David was one of the one in ten who had a chance of being healed. He put him on cortisone and other medication and constantly monitored his condition.

David had several attacks in those first years in Florida. It seems that every time we thought he had it licked, he'd get another attack and have to get back on cortisone. As a result of the disease, he missed out on football, baseball and all those other sports.

He graduated from high school, worked for a couple of years and met and married a wonderful young woman. Then, against my loudest protestations, he decided to join the Army. I told him he was crazy to want to go into the Army, even if they accepted him. Such a rigorous life would kill him. Besides, I could not see my son in a position in which someone could tell him to kill. He tried to join, but when he told them about the disease, they sent him home.

I was elated but the elation was short-lived. Three months later, David tried again. This time, they didn't ask him any questions in which he had to admit his disease. They accepted him. I was livid.

On the day David left for boot camp, I drove him to the bus station. As the bus pulled away, I stood there and cried. All I could see was a one-year-old baby strapped to a plank, crying for water. Then I decided to catch up to the bus, to wave farewell one more time, but I couldn't close the distance.

When I got back home, Peg and I sat and cried. And we continued to pray.

That was twenty-five years ago. David never had another

attack of Bright's Disease. He took on the tough jobs in the Army. He joined the airborne Rangers, jumped out of perfectly good airplanes and was in a special services units, which does dangerous jobs such as hostage rescues. He became an instructor at West Point and earned every peacetime honor possible.

Today, Command Sergeant Major David J. Libersat is at Fort Benning, Georgia, where, in his words, he continues to serve his country as a peacekeeper.

When Doubt Was Wiped Away

Since Halloween of 1976, I have been living a new life of freedom, joy and purpose, a life with clarity of mind and vision.

I still have my problems. I still fight with ego, the drive to control everything, the tenacious clinging to possessions, the fiery temper, the relentless temptation. So what is there to be so happy about?

God loves me. He loves you. Of this I am very sure, although I was not always so sure. In fact, I didn't really believe God could love me. In spite of being loved by my family and fellow Christians, I thought I was unworthy of love. If someone did actually love me, it was only because that person didn't really know me.

That feeling led me to seek solace in alcohol. I was eventually healed of alcoholism, but that is another story. Before defeating alcohol, I had to experience a deep, deep healing, one that went to the core of my soul, one that left me weeping, even shouting for joy.

I had been a Catholic journalist for seventeen years. Peg and I had been married twenty-four years, and all seven children were born and growing into the fine people they are today. We had a large family, a small income and financial problems. We even considered bankruptcy on more than one occasion, but we "hung in there."

There was a deep sadness in me. I was lonely. Even in the midst of family or at Mass I felt alone, left out. I suppose some of the things I experienced as a child contributed to this feeling. I was the proverbial ninety-pound weakling. I couldn't keep up with other boys my age and was a klutz in sports. I was something of a "mama's boy" and a typical nerd—all brains with eyes set on visions of the future. I thought that most people lived shallow and unfocused lives.

I really suffered for all that but, in retrospect, I realize that I brought a lot of the pain on myself. I considered myself better than others, and I really liked being above what they considered fun or important.

At any rate, in 1976 I was forty-two, unhappy, hooked on alcohol, angry at the world and blaming others for my problems.

In 1969, we had lived briefly in Indiana. While there, I had heard of "Catholic Pentecostals" and read the book by the same name written by Kevin and Dorothy Ranaghan. I had talked with people who experienced a revival of faith through what they called the "baptism of the Holy Spirit."

I remember thinking, "This is wonderful. I wish something like that could happen to me." As a child, I had listened to Bible stories about how the Apostles worked miracles. I always wondered, "If it's the same church and the same God, why aren't those things happening today?" Now, I was hearing that such things did happen today and to many people, Catholic and otherwise.

Through some friends active in the Catholic charismatic renewal, I heard of Sister Briege McKenna, a Franciscan nun with a special gift of healing. One day, I was editing a story about Sister Briege submitted by one of our writers. The story stayed on my desk for a number of weeks and I read it from time to time. The story reported that she prayed with people over the phone and they were healed. I called her.

Naturally, I didn't tell her that my real problem was that I felt unloved. In fact, I'm not sure I realized that was my problem. And I was not ready to admit to myself or anyone else that I was an alcoholic. I just said that I had trouble surrendering to God and that I wanted to grow in faith. Actually, I was green with envy of those Catholics who had found such a close, personal relationship with Jesus and, as a result, led such happy and fruitful lives.

Sister Briege prayed with me. Nothing happened. I wanted a miracle of grace and nothing happened. But her prayer did touch me. I felt drawn to Sister Briege, she seemed so at home with God. Maybe, I thought, if I can't get close to God I can at least get closer to people who are close to God.

I wrote to Sr. Briege and called her often. Eventually, I met her in person and she prayed with me again. It was October 31, 1976.

As she prayed she thanked God for me, for Peg and the kids, for my gift of writing and my work in the church. She asked God to bless my marriage and to make Peg and me strong in faith.

As Sister Briege prays with people, the Lord gives her images. She may not understand the significance of what she sees in her spirit but she shares the images and usually they mean much to those to whom she is ministering.

She said, "I see you

> ## *Prayer of Intercession*
>
> Intercession is a prayer of petition that leads us to pray as Jesus did. He is the one intercessor with the Father on behalf of all men, especially sinners. He is "able for all time to save those who draw near to God through him, since he always lives to make intercession for them" (Heb 7:25, RSV).... In intercession, he who prays looks "not only to his own interests, but also to the interests of others," even to the point of praying for those who do him harm (Phil 2:4, RSV; cf. Rom 12:14, 10:1); Catechism of the Catholic Church, No. 2634-35).

all alone." Immediately I thought, "That figures; nobody loves me." Then she said, "I see you alone but you are with the Lord. The Lord is saying, 'That child of yours that you and your wife have been praying for, don't worry about him, my arm is around him and he is all right.'" Only an insight from God could have revealed this since I had not told her of this family crisis.

I was suddenly aware of a great peace, a warmth, a profound

presence. I burst into tears and began to sob uncontrollably. She was holding my hands and my nose was running like Niagara Falls, but I was not about to let go of her hands. She was a vital connection with God who, at that moment, was with us in a profound way.

She continued to pray. After a bit, she said, "I see you with the Lord again. He has his arm around you and he is telling you, 'That person who has turned his back on everyone and on the church, don't worry about him, my arm is around him and he is all right.'" Again, she had no earthly way of knowing this. I wept even harder. God did know me. He knew what was hurting me so deeply. It was as though every bit of pain and sorrow was being pulled out of me.

And still she prayed: "I see you on a mountaintop and the Lord is with you. On the side of the mountain there are people who want to come up to where you are so they can be with the Lord. But they are frightened. They feel unwanted, like those sick with leprosy in the Scriptures. They run into the shadows and hide behind rocks because they are afraid.

"Henry, the Lord is calling you to a great work."

I had never in my life felt so light, so full, so free, so peaceful, so joyful. I thanked Sister Briege. We both knew that this was the beginning of a life far different from the one I had been living up to that moment.

I don't know how I did it, but I managed to drive home from that meeting. I don't know what people thought of me, or why some state patrolman didn't pull me over. I drove with my car window down and my head out the window, shouting to God and everybody, "It's true! It's true! It's true!"

It is true! God loves me! And he loves you. He will answer your prayer just as he answered mine.

A year later, I was healed of alcoholism. For many years, I thought kicking alcohol was my real healing. It was not. The real healing was the spiritual one God accomplished on Halloween in 1976. All the spooks were going to leave me. The Holy Spirit had moved in.

God Hears Other's Prayers

Since God intervened in my life, he has used me to bring healing to other alcoholics. Here are four of those stories.

In September 1977, I had been healed of my addiction to alcohol. A few months later, I told my story at the King of Kings Prayer Group of Sts. Peter and Paul Parish in Goldenrod, Florida. At the end of the meeting, the leaders and I prayed for people.

A woman approached and said she had a dear friend who was addicted to alcohol, and she wanted to "stand in" for her friend. I took her hands and prayed, "Lord Jesus, please use this woman's love for her friend as an avenue of your healing power. Heal her, Lord, of this terrible addiction even as you healed me."

Some weeks later, I was invited back to the prayer group. The same woman came to me and asked, "Did you hear what happened?" I said I had not.

She said, "Three days after we prayed for my friend, she came up to me and said that when she woke up two days ago—the day after we prayed for her—she lost all desire to drink!"

A year later, the woman told me her friend was still sober and going to AA regularly.

* * *

Another time, I preached at all the Masses at St. James Cathedral in Orlando. I shared the story of how I had been healed, and spoke of God's desire to heal. Some time later, I was praying privately in the cathedral when a woman I recognized from the local prayer group tapped me on the shoulder.

"I just wanted you to know," she said, "that when I heard you preach on your healing and on God's love, I was deeply moved. The next day I went to an Alcoholics Anonymous meeting and I haven't had a drink since. I go to two meetings each day and I take one day at a time."

Two years later, she was still sober, but I have not seen her since.

* * *

Preaching God's word with expectant faith evokes a faithful response in those who hear it. I was a speaker for the annual charismatic conference for the Diocese of Camden, New Jersey. I again shared my story.

During a break, a woman approached and asked me to pray for her husband. We asked God to heal him of his addiction to alcohol. Later, during the same conference, a man came for prayer. He, too, was an alcoholic. We prayed.

Two years later, when I was again a speaker at the conference the man who had personally asked for prayer told me he was healed and attending AA.

Four years after that first conference, I spoke at the archdiocesan charismatic conference in Philadelphia. The woman who had asked for prayer for her husband during that first Camden conference told me her husband had stopped drinking entirely.

SIX

Two Major Healings

Bob Kinsey, 64, a deacon in the Diocese of Orlando, Florida, thinks he is very blessed. He is grateful to God for not one, but two healings. One, a healing from cancer, combined prayer and chemotherapy. The other, when he was healed of Guillain-Barré Syndrome, brought statements of amazement from doctors and nurses.

He was forty-two years old and in the Marine Corps Reserve when he went in for his regular four-year checkup. The doctors did a complete examination including a chest x-ray that revealed that he had a widening of the media stynum. He asked them, "What's the media stynum?" They explained it was the column of tissue behind the breastbone, and in his case it had expanded into a mass that could be quite serious.

When the doctors compared their x-ray to an earlier one, they decided to x-ray him yet again. Finally, they said they wanted to "go in and see what was going on." Bob said, "Define going in."

The doctors performed a media scenoptiky, going into the chest cavity through the throat and snipping a piece out of the media stynum. That was in January of 1977.

Three days later, the surgeon went to Bob's room, and with "great bedside manner" said, "By the way, we got the lab report and you have Hodgkin's disease." The doctor then walked out the door.

Bob was not a happy camper. What was Hodgkin's disease? How bad was it? What did they plan to do about it? What were his options? What was the prognosis?

He asked a nurse but she was very reluctant to answer his questions. She finally said another doctor, a hematologist, would be in to talk to him. He was the one to give Bob the news: "You have cancer." Bob was crushed and frightened.

Immediately, the doctors said they wanted to remove his spleen. Bob refused because he had had all kinds of tests that showed there was no cancer anywhere else. He was told that the spleen acts as a reservoir for cancer cells and that the spleen had to come out. Bob wanted a second opinion. The doctor was "absolutely livid," and said, in effect, "Well, you do what you want to do!" And Bob said, "Darn right I will, it's my body!" Then Bob asked him, "If you were me and wanted a second opinion, where would you go?" The doctor wouldn't give Bob a reference.

Bob and Joan had friends in New York who put them in touch with the Sloan-Kettering Cancer Research Center there. Bob went to Sloan-Kettering and was told that "we don't take out spleens anymore." The doctors, after looking over all of

Bob's medical records, decided that a larger biopsy was needed to determine to which stage his disease had progressed. In Florida, he had been diagnosed as a Stage One-A patient. In New York, it was determined that he was close to Stage Four. Stage Five is the worst possible stage. The cancer was beginning to reach out to other organs.

Bob returned to Florida and began a course of intensive chemotherapy that was "unpleasant, to say the least." He took the treatment for six months. It was during this period, in the spring of 1977, that Sister Briege came to minister at a healing service in the Kinseys' home parish, St. Peter's. She spoke at all Masses and invited everyone to come to a healing service that Sunday afternoon.

Bob left Mass with no intention of going to the service. He was down and feeling bad and was skeptical about such things. Joan asked if they would attend and Bob said no.

The healing service was at two in the afternoon and at fifteen minutes before two, Bob was all dressed up. Joan asked him where he was going. "We're going to the healing service," Bob told her. It was there that Bob felt the healing presence and promise of God.

Sister Briege, "in her low-key way," gave a little talk on healing, he said. She was not at all what Bob expected after having heard about and seeing some "healers" in action.

Sister Briege invited everyone to come up and form a line before the sanctuary. Bob and Joan stood side by side. Neither Bob nor Joan had spoken to Sister Briege and she didn't know he had cancer. Nor did she know about his recent operation in which the doctors cut through the right side of his chest to take the larger piece of tissue.

Here is Bob's experience in his own words.

"She moved down the line and kind of laid her hand on each person's head and said something like, 'May the Lord heal you' and whatever else came to her mind. Joan was on my left and another person was on my right. She prayed over Joan first, then over me. She laid her hand on my head and prayed and went on to the person on my right.

"But before she put her hand on his head, she came back to me. She put her hand on my chest, right where the incision was. She put her hand *right over the incision, right over that spot,* and she said, 'May the Lord continue to heal you.'

"She didn't know me from Adam's house cat. Needless to say, I was blubbering. Joan and I were both crying. I knew, without a doubt, it was a touch from God. She is truly an instrument of the Lord."

Bob didn't stop taking treatments. But, he said, "I just took Sister Briege's prayer as a confirmation that I would be healed. Throughout the illness, I was convinced we could beat this thing. That's a gift I have. Let's do what we have to do and carry on. Whatever happens, happens.

"I finished the chemotherapy in August. In September, I went back into an Orlando hospital and they repeated all the tests. On the third day, the oncologist came up and told me, 'We can find no trace of cancer.'

"I'm sure it was the touch, the hand of the Lord, the chemo—all of that was part of my cure. Since 1977 to this day in 1998, I have had no trace of cancer. At that time, I also had a sense of God having some more work for me to do. One day, my pastor tapped me on the shoulder and said he wanted me to begin training for the diaconate." Bob thought the pastor "had gone out of his mind," and told him so. The pastor, Father Nolin, said, "Just try it."

Bob and Joan agreed and they went through three years of training. Bob was ordained. Today, still an active insurance agent, he is co-director of the Office of the Diaconate in the Diocese of Orlando. He is very active in St. Peter's parish, and a man who is widely respected in both religious and secular circles.

And, yes, God was not through with him in the health category as well. Bob was to experience the power of prayer and God's healing love yet another time.

In 1992, he contracted Guillain-Barré Syndrome, a debilitating disease that leads to loss of muscle strength and sometimes paralysis. Without warning, on a Sunday afternoon, he began to feel numbness in his fingers and then in his hands. On Monday morning, the numbness was also in his feet. He didn't think anything of it and went to work.

As the day progressed, he noticed it became harder and harder to walk. His feet were heavy and he felt flat-footed. On Tuesday morning, he drove to a work-related appointment and on his way home had trouble operating the car's stick shift. When he got home, he called Joan at her job and asked her to take him to the doctor.

The family doctor, a general practitioner, said he had a

God Heals Through Doctors

From God the doctor has his wisdom, and the king provides for his sustenance.

His knowledge makes the doctor distinguished, and gives him access to those in authority.

Then give the doctor his place lest he leave; for you need him too.

There are times that give him an advantage, and he too beseeches God that his diagnosis may be correct and his treatment bring about a cure.

He who is a sinner toward his Maker will be defiant toward the doctor (Sir 38:2-3, 12-15).

"descending neuropathy." Bob said, "Really?" The doctor immediately sent him to a neurologist. This specialist wanted Bob to go into the hospital right away for tests, but Bob declined. The doctor said that if Bob experienced any trouble breathing he should rush right to the emergency room.

The next morning, Bob was so weak that Joan had to help him out of bed. She put him on the couch with a phone nearby. Then she left for St. Peter's School where she works as principal. By noon, Bob was so weak he couldn't walk and realized he needed to get to the hospital. He called Joan and a friend carried him from the house to the car and from the car to the wheelchair that brought him into the hospital.

After numerous tests, the doctor said, "You have Guillain-Barré Syndrome." No one knows exactly what triggers Guillain-Barré Syndrome, but it is a disorder in which the body's immune system attacks the sheath surrounding nerve endings. Impulses from the nerve endings to the brain are unable to get through.

The doctor began massive doses of gamma globulin. That was Friday, and by Sunday Bob couldn't move at all. He couldn't feed himself, dress himself or do anything for himself.

With this disease, Bob explained, "You go down very fast and then you level out. Healing can be very rapid or very slow." After the gamma globulin, the doctor began rigorous physical therapy. After two weeks, Bob was transferred to Sand Lake Hospital, a rehabilitation facility with an excellent reputation in physical therapy. Joan Marie, their daughter, worked there and took over Bob's care.

He was an inpatient at Sand Lake for five weeks. Every day, he was given physical and speech therapy. "They make a video of you on the first day of physical therapy to record motor responses. My video," Bob said, "was pathetic."

Bob was helpless, unable to meet his most private hygiene needs. Today, he quips, "I don't know, but maybe the Lord was telling me I need more humility."

After only five weeks, he was allowed to go home. He explains his rapid recovery in these words: "To no credit of my own, I am known as a sort of legend at that place. They had never seen anyone my age come back that fast. Without a doubt, it was prayer. I had thousands of people praying for me. The whole diaconate community at home and those in other dioceses were praying. Prisoners on a Kairos retreat I was supposed to have worked at, a Cursillo I was supposed to have helped with, people in my parish, family and friends throughout the nation—they were all praying for me."

Bob got to the hospital in October. He was asked by the therapist, "What are your goals, Mr. Kinsey?" She pushed him for specific goals. "OK," he said, "I have a plane ticket to go skiing in Montana in February. I want to make that trip." She pushed further, "What else?" Bob said, "My other passion in life is to play tennis. I want to be on the tennis court in April, close to where I was before I got sick. My other passion is I want to be back at the altar as soon as possible. Those are my three goals."

Even though he was not up to snuff in the sporting activities, he made all three goals in the time limits he had set. "Without a doubt, it was the power of prayer and God's goodness," says Deacon Bob Kinsey.

SEVEN

The Jesse Tree

In Advent of 1997, our parish put up a Jesse Tree in the parish chapel. A Jesse Tree is a small bare tree or large, bare branch that symbolizes life before the saving life, death and resurrection of Jesus. Traditionally, Jesse Trees are decorated with symbols from the Old Testament such as Jacob's ladder or the Star of David or Noah's Ark.

That year, our associate pastor, Father Ed Thompson, invited parishioners to put a Christmas ornament on the tree representing someone who was sick or alienated from the church or in need in other ways. Our pastor, Father Charles Mitchell, encouraged us to pray for all these individual intentions. The entire parish prayed at every Mass for all the people represented on the Jesse Tree and many parishioners interceded for the intentions in their private prayer time.

What happened was wonderful! Here are three stories about prayers being answered.

Prayer Overcomes Alienation

Richard and Doris had relatives, Lucille and Roger, who lived "up north." They had been away from the church for forty years. The couple had become alienated when Lucille had a hysterectomy and confessed this to a priest. The priest didn't give her absolution and told her to go home and think about what she had done. She went but, with Roger, felt pushed away from the church.

A few years before the parish Jesse Tree, Lucille and Roger had visited their Florida relatives for several months. Richard and Doris brought them to Mass on Christmas and Easter. It was the first time the couple had been to church in many years.

Lucille and Roger were deeply touched by the warmth, openness and joy in our parish. They were especially moved by the baptism of adults at the Easter vigil Mass. The couple then returned to their home up north.

When the parish set up the Jesse Tree, Richard and Doris put an ornament on the tree representing Lucille and Roger. Their prayer was that they would return to the church. They didn't mention this to their relatives. Doris and Richard also sent their relatives' names to the Missionary Oblates of Mary Immaculate at Our Lady of the Snows national shrine in Belleview, Illinois.

Later, Richard and Doris learned that Lucille and Roger went to church on Christmas Day, 1997. A few months later, Roger died of lung cancer. Lucille herself has suffered clogged arteries and has had two separate surgeries for that condition.

The doctors took blood vessels from her legs to help repair her arteries but long after the last surgery, her legs remained painful.

Lucille became depressed with the burden of ill health. As though this were not enough, her daughter died suddenly. Doris feared for her relative. Could Lucille weather still another tragic blow?

She could and did. Lucille is still making her way back into active Catholic life, but in spite of illness, she experiences an inner peace, even joy. And she is eager when people offer to pray with her.

Hers is a gradual spiritual healing. God calls and beckons, but he doesn't force himself on anyone. He always honors a person's free will and is willing to wait as people work their way, sometimes slowly, back into his embrace and that of his Church.

Mary Is Singing Again

One parishioner, Lillian, has a sister who had been away from the church for eleven years. Mary became alienated from the church and even from God when her husband died shortly after he had been diagnosed with Lou Gehrig's disease.

For three years, doctors had been treating him for arthritis and had failed to diagnose his condition accurately. Mary was angry with the doctors, and when her husband died, she became angry with God. She felt alone and lived as though oblivious to everything. In Lillian's words, "She sort of hibernated."

Previously, Mary had been very active in church, singing at weddings, funerals and at Mass on Sundays. Lillian placed an ornament on the Jesse Tree for Mary and continued "to pray very hard for her."

On Christmas Eve, 1997, Mary's grandson was an altar server at the children's Mass. She attended and sang along with the choir and congregation.

A gentleman sitting next to her said, "You have a beautiful voice, why don't you do something with it?" She said, "Well, I used to." He said, "Why don't you do it again?"

And she did. On Christmas Day, Mary called Lillian to tell her she had gone to church. Mary was "amazed at all the beauty she had been missing for all those years."

Mary is still going to Mass. She is still singing for the Lord.

"Just One Day, Lord, Just One Day"

Two sisters put an ornament on the Jesse Tree for their mother who was suffering from Alzheimer's disease. They prayed that she would be "her old self" for just one day. They so longed to be with their mother as she had been before the disease struck.

Their prayer was answered—on Christmas Day! They shared that holy day with their mother, who was very lucid. Then she slipped away again. But they had that one, wonderful gift from God on Christmas Day.

EIGHT

He Was Healed Without Even Asking

‡══‡

Monsignor Irving A. DeBlanc, now in his eighties, is still an active priest in the Diocese of Lake Charles, Louisiana. When most people want to sit back and rest on their laurels, he is actively pursuing a new ministry to the people of the "Third Age." He doesn't like the term "senior citizens" because it has become synonymous with stockpiled grey-headed people considered has-beens. He sees great possibilities for people of age.

For as long as I have known him—since 1952, when he was a college chaplain—Father DeBlanc has never been one to talk about himself. He has been a man for others—even in high positions such as National Family Life Director for the United States' bishops.

So it was most unusual, when I told him about this book of Catholic healing stories, that he volunteered, "I had a healing at Medjugorje." Msgr. DeBlanc visited the site of the widely acclaimed Marian apparitions and, to his surprise, was invited to be the principal celebrant at a Mass.

He had been suffering from an ulcer behind his ear and the earpiece of his eyeglasses constantly irritated the sore. "I had begun to place the earpiece on the outside of my ear so the ulcer would not be irritated and painful. But this was a distraction for people. So, after proclaiming the gospel and preaching, I decided that for the Eucharistic Prayer, I would wear my glasses properly and just bear the pain. I didn't want any distractions at Mass.

"When I put my glasses on, I was totally surprised to realize there was no pain. The ulcer was completely gone. After months and months of medicines and doctor visits to no avail, God healed the ulcer through Our Lady's intercession at Medjugorje."

NINE

Healings Both Marvelous and Humorous

She's known worldwide as Auntie Babsie. Nearing eighty years of age, she travels around the world preaching the gospel and calling God's people to greater faith. She has the gifts of prophecy, discernment and healing.

Babsie Bleasdell is her name, and her native land is Trinidad. We met in Cape May, New Jersey where we were speakers at an annual conference of the Camden Diocese's charismatic renewal. For me, it was love at first sight. Auntie Babsie is genuine.

In her beautiful book, Refresh Your Life in the Spirit, *she tells several healing stories. Her book and her ministry focus on being totally converted to Christ, embracing, as Catholics, the Way, the Truth and the Life, and following the teachings of the magisterium.*

Auntie Babsie has shown through example and word how people can grow in faith and in the power of the Spirit by following faithfully the teachings of the Church. She combines traditional with charismatic, doctrine with prayer and faith with daily life. In that context, she has graciously given us permission to share stories from Refresh Your Life in the Spirit. *As you will see from her words and examples, Auntie Babsie is "down to earth."*

A Mute Child Is Healed

Auntie Babsie tells the story of Mary Goddard, a Pentecostal who ministered to the fledgling Catholic charismatics in Trinidad many years ago. In a weeklong seminar, Mary had given the large group of Catholics a complete orientation to the workings and power of the Holy Spirit. Some time later, Mary came back to Trinidad to minister. During a healing service, a mother brought forward her twelve-year-old daughter who was screaming uncontrollably. The mother said to Auntie Babsie, "I want you to pray for this child."

Auntie Babsie, still new in her experience with the Lord, said, "Let Mary pray for her." The mother replied, "No, I want you to pray for her."

Auntie Babsie said to herself, "Lord, what am I to do? I don't know what to do!" Then she asked the mother, "Why is your child screaming?" She replied, "Never mind that, she's just afraid of the crowd. Just pray for her." Auntie Babsie asked her what was wrong with the child. The mother answered, "She can't speak."

So Auntie Babsie laid hands on the child's throat and prayed. "I spoke to her vocal chords in the name of Jesus, asking Jesus to heal her. Then I prayed for peace for the child and her screaming subsided."

The next day, Auntie Babsie left the country for a couple of weeks abroad. When she returned she went to the cathedral to pray.

"The mother had been searching for me and found me there. I asked, 'How is your child?' The mother said, 'She speaks!'" And she told Auntie Babsie she had a gift for her and wanted to bring the little girl to see her. She told the mother, "I have no need for a gift but I would happily see the child."

The mother brought the child to Auntie Babsie's home and, seeing the woman who had prayed for her, the child shouted: "Babsie!"

Auntie Babsie recounts: "I was surprised at first. In my country, children are taught to address their elders with respect; even old people call me 'Auntie Babsie.' And this child called me 'Babsie.' Laughing, I said to the child, 'You have the right to call me "Babsie!"' I was humbled to realize that through this little child God had taught me to be open to his gift of healing."

> ## "Ephphatha! ... Be Opened"
>
> Some people brought him a deaf man who had a speech impediment and begged him to lay his hand on him. Jesus took him off by himself away from the crowd. He put his fingers into the man's ears and, spitting, touched his tongue; then he looked up to heaven and emitted a groan. He said to him, "Ephphatha!" (that is, "Be opened!") At once the man's ears were opened; he was freed from the impediment, and began to speak plainly. Then he enjoined them strictly not to tell anyone; but the more he ordered them not to, the more they proclaimed it. Their amazement went beyond all bounds: "He has done everything well! He makes the deaf hear and the mute speak!" (Mk 7:32-37).

An Embarrassment and a Healing

One of the gifts of the Holy Spirit given for the sake of others is the gift of knowledge. Through this gift, God reveals something that has not been learned naturally—from others or from reading.

Auntie Babsie tells about an embarrassed man, a "revelation" and a down-to-earth healing.

"We were at a large teaching session on the word of knowledge in South Trinidad. I had gone there in extreme pain. It isn't very dignified, but I have to tell you, I had a severe attack of hemorrhoids. Nobody knew. It was so bad it was like I was eating pain day and night. As I was helping to support people in prayer, a man participating in the seminar said, 'I have a strange thing to say. I am ashamed and embarrassed to say it.' I asked him what it was. He said, 'Somebody here is suffering with hemorrhoids.' I laughed in surprise and said in jest, 'Gee, you didn't have to take my pants down in public!' At this, the poor man blushed and he suggested I should get Mary to pray for me. I said, 'No, it's your word of knowledge. God will give you the power to pray and to bring healing.'

"I said to him, 'Come on, now. You can't let me down. You've stimulated my hope that I could get some relief from my pain.' I suffered with this affliction from time to time. It would just come upon me. As embarrassed as he was, he prayed with me. From that day in 1978 to this very day I have never had another attack. Immediately I got relief and it has never returned.

"God used this man, as embarrassed as he was and as incompetent as he felt. God gave him the word of knowledge and heard his prayer to give me a permanent healing. That's what can happen when people put their faith in God, their expectant faith."

TEN

Never An Unanswered Prayer

They both chuckle as James says, "We were both born in Wilmington." And Lois chimes in, "He was born in Wilmington, Delaware, and I was born in Wilmington, North Carolina."

James and Lois Phillips are those wonderful and beautiful kind of people who make waves without jumping up and down in the water. They are quiet and deeply in love with one another. Their faith is almost tangible. You need only speak with them a few minutes to experience a certain calming spirit. They shun the limelight and you never hear a word of complaint or criticism from them.

Now in their eighties, married more than sixty-three years, they have nine children, seventeen grandchildren and thirty-two great-grandchildren, with "another great-grandchild on the way." As James puts it, "We're old enough to have a retired son and daughter."

They have experienced heartache, suffering and serious illness. But, as Lois attests, she never has a doubt that God hears and answers prayer. She says, with engaging simplicity, "I have never had a prayer that went unanswered." Perhaps it's that simplicity that makes their story of faith so credible.

It was faith that led them to a charismatic prayer group where they experienced an ever-deepening relationship with God and their fellow Christians. Their parish prayer group is "what really helped us grow in faith—praying together and seeing so many prayers answered." She says with emphasis, "And we do nothing but pray. I believe in the power of prayer. I believe that if people get together like that, God will hear them."

She looks back on the years. "If it were not for prayer, my daughter, Francine, would not be here today." As an adult, Francine suffered from headaches. Her doctors, after thorough examinations, could find nothing wrong. Finally, after much prayer and Francine's insistence that there was a problem, the doctors administered an MRI. They discovered that she had several veins in her brain that were isolated from other vessels. The condition, which had been present from birth, caused blood to collect in the area and remain there. They urgently recommended surgery.

The procedure was supposed to take four hours, "but six hours later," Lois said, "they were still in there. We were really getting scared and we continued to pray. The surgery lasted six and a half hours because when they got into the brain, they discovered a total of seventeen such veins. The condition had already caused an aneurysm."

The surgery was successful, but how could they be sure the happy outcome was due to prayer and not the skill of the doctors?

"Oh, the skill of the doctors had a lot to do with the success of the surgery," Lois explains. "If God had not been watching over her, they would have never found the problem. The doctors said that had she not persisted with her complaint and if the problem had not been discovered, she was ready for a stroke and would have died."

Lois says that Francine, for her part, knows that prayer is the reason she is here today. "The entire experience helped her understand better the power of prayer. She says that had it not been for the prayers of people from the church and her job, she never would have made it."

How is Francine today? Fine, say the parents, and helping her daughter prepare for her wedding. She has to return to the doctor for an annual checkup, but there have been no symptoms to cause any concern.

Lois tells of their son who was born with clubfeet so deformed that the soles of his feet turned upward. His legs were put in casts when he was five days old and he stayed in the hospital for three months. After many visits to doctors and hospitals, finally, says Lois, they "prayed the child into a hospital that didn't take such cases." Then they prayed for and found a doctor who would tackle the delicate surgery on the baby's heel tendons. Prayer, both James and Lois insist, played a major role in that child's healing. Doctors said he would never walk, but through surgery and prayer, the condition was corrected. Today, their son is nearly sixty years old and has never had a problem walking. Lois says he knows of the healing he received, but he was so young that it had no appreciable effect on his faith life.

The Phillips' experience of God's healing power does not end there. Lois herself experienced a healing through prayer, and one for which doctors can take no credit.

In 1997, Lois went for her regular mammogram and she knew "something was up" when the nurse led her to another room. A doctor came in and told her she had a lump in her

What Are They Doing, Putting Hands on Her Head?

A mother caresses her sick child's forehead as she prays for a fever to break. Doctors and nurses know that touching someone is comforting. Someone lays a hand on another person's shoulder—a sign of support, affection, sympathy.

It is an ancient Christian custom to "lay hands" on people as you pray for them. Priests and other ministers to sick people know that respectfully and reverently touching a sick person is a sign of God's love for them. It is a way to physically demonstrate the heartfelt desire for the Holy Spirit to impart the gift of healing. Touching in love and sympathy is a natural gesture. Grace builds on nature. While doing what comes naturally, prayer brings added meaning to the natural gesture of touching.

breast and recommended a biopsy. Several x-rays and another mammogram confirmed that the lump was there. Lois made an appointment for the biopsy.

Their close friends were praying for Lois, and she was included in the parish's general intercessions at Mass. "On Monday night," Lois says, "we went to the prayer meeting. We met in the Blessed Mother Grotto ... she's my favorite. She has never yet refused a favor I've asked of her. I've prayed to her all my life. Everyone placed hands on me and prayed for me and for the procedure which was scheduled for the next morning. I came out of there feeling really good, like a load had been taken off my shoulders."

Lois went to the hospital the next morning. For three hours, they took more x-rays, more mammograms and conducted more tests. "They couldn't find the lump," Lois smiles. "The doctor seemed very upset and embarrassed. She said, 'I don't understand this. It was there.' I said, 'Yes, Ma'am, I know.' The doctor said, 'I just don't know what to do. Well, go home and in three months, go back for another mammogram and see what happens.'"

Lois said, "I did. And I go every three months. And there is still no lump."

ELEVEN

She Didn't Want to Be Healed

Heidi Hess shares two stories that, really, are parts of the same story of God's action in her life. Heidi is an editor at Servant Publications. We have had the pleasure of working together. In a conversation about a project, she told me she had experienced a marvelous healing.

When she was seventeen, Heidi was in a terrible automobile accident. In addition to her extensive internal injuries, her leg was crushed and required surgery. A pin was used to hold her bones together. Doctors told her it would be at least a year before she would walk again.

One Sunday, a friend asked Heidi, at that time a Protestant Evangelical, to attend a charismatic church service with him. At the church service, the pastor prayed over Heidi. He pushed on her head, "trying to push me down," she said. (The minister was "encouraging" her to "rest in the Spirit," a phenomenon that can be a true gift from God in a healing moment.) However, Heidi wasn't about to fake anything, so the pastor leading the service abruptly sent her back to her seat. She was turned off by the experience and came to doubt any possibility of instananeous healing through prayer.

Six months later, Heidi was well enough to move to Minneapolis to attend Bible school. But just a few months into her first semester there, the pin in her leg slipped, causing her excruciating pain. X-rays revealed that the pin was rubbing against part of the bone. The doctors would have to operate again. Two days before she was scheduled to have the surgery, she heard a knock on the door. In walked a deacon from her church and his wife.

"May we pray with you for healing?" the deacon asked. Heidi was hesitant, but he insisted, "I believe God will heal you if you have faith. I want you to stand up."

Heidi thought he was nuts. She could hardly stand the pain simply lying in bed. "I can't stand up," she said. But the deacon insisted.

"I decided to just put my toe on the floor. At the first twinge I was going to scream loud enough to wake up the entire building." She put a toe on the floor. No pain. "I decided to gently put my entire foot on the floor. Surely that would bring both the pain and the scream." No pain. She sensed a faint "click" in her hip joint, but there was no other sensation.

Heidi chuckles, "I found myself bouncing around trying to make it hurt but there was no pain." After an x-ray, she and her doctors discovered that the pin had slipped back into place. The film showed clearly where the pin had worn away at the bone when it was out of place.

One more operation and the pin was gone and Heidi was on her way. "After that, I finished Bible school and did mission work. I felt I had to do something to repay God for what he had done for me.

"However, I got so caught up in doing things for God that I suffered burnout. Then my father became ill, and I realized that my spiritual 'bank' had been almost completely depleted. I spent about a year in which I felt apart from God and was inactive in church. One day, I realized that something had to change. I decided to drop in at the nearest church. It happened to be a Catholic church."

And here begins the second part of her story. Heidi said that while she sat there during Mass, "I felt very peaceful. I didn't understand what was going on—the liturgy, the vestments, the flow of the service. The Catholic Church is a little hard to break into," she laughed. "But as I continued going to that church, I felt more and more peace. Finally I decided it was time to talk to the RCIA director." (RCIA stands for Rite of Christian Initiation for Adults, the program used throughout the Church to help people who want to enter the Catholic faith.)

"It took me about a year and a half to finally make the decision to join the Church. At first, I didn't like considering myself a convert. After all, I had accepted Jesus long before, when I was just a child. But, you know, becoming a Catholic is a conversion process. You have to have a complete mind change.

"I had gotten into doing all the right things, having all the right answers. I could quote verse after verse of Scripture—and my spiritual pride really got me into trouble. Now I had to rethink my relationship with God and others as well as my understanding of the Bible. It was a humbling experience, which was exactly what I needed at that time.

"One of the things that had to change was my understanding of suffering. I had been under the impression that God does not allow his children to suffer, and that suffering was usually evidence of some moral flaw in a suffering person's life. As a Catholic, I came to understand that suffering can play a vital role in our spiritual maturity.

"When God first healed my leg I argued with him for months afterward. There were others who needed his help much more than I had at the time: children dying from leukemia, grandmothers from breast cancer, fathers from heart disease. I had been scheduled for surgery that would have alleviated my pain in just a few days. But God saw fit to heal me sooner.

"Looking back, I think God was trying to show me how different his eternal perspective is from ours. That small lesson in obedience—standing up even though I knew it would hurt—prepared me for much more difficult choices still ahead of me. His comforting arms held me up at every step. And they continue to hold me—to hold all of us—to this day."

TWELVE

A Layman Reports Healings in Ministry

———✦———

The following reports were first printed in The Shepherd's Voice, *the newsletter of the Children of God Prayer Community of St. Luke's parish, Stockton, California. Robert Canton, a lay leader of the community, has a healing ministry.*

Dr. Mary, as we will call her, is a pediatrician practicing in her island home, a possession of the United States. When Dr. Mary had been practicing for about thirteen years, a routine chest x-ray gave evidence of a lung tumor. A CT scan revealed that it was benign and posed no danger of incapacitation or imminent death.

But Dr. Mary met a new enemy: fear.

The situation, Dr. Mary said, "gave birth to fear of dying and of leaving my three children motherless. Intellectual clarity gave way to panic. Time was now a luxury and a precious commodity. Death seemed to be lurking everywhere." She began to concentrate on making money to provide for her "future orphans." Fear clouded her judgment and made her believe she was deathly ill in spite of medical evidence to the contrary.

In the process of concentrating on death and on making money, Mary said that "anger, resentment and blaming others—including God—led to spiritual death. Spiritual poverty had crept into family relations."

In October of 1994, she suffered severe asthma that confined her to bed and rendered her all but voiceless. She telephoned her sister, whom we will call Liza, who lives in California. She asked Liza to pray for her and for another sister who suffered from a mild stroke. Liza had grown close to God. She prayed for Mary over the phone and said she would ask Bob Canton, a lay minister, to pray for them.

"Sometime later," Dr. Mary said, "I woke up early in the morning to make my regular meditation. As soon as I opened my eyes, there appeared an image of the Holy Spirit, visible from my bed, and it seemed to be hazy. Surrounding it was a rosary of stars—like diamonds in a crown. The image lasted for less than a minute. I gave no significance to it, attributing it to a half-awake, dreamlike state."

A few days later, Liza called her sister, Mary, and informed her that Robert Canton had prayed for her. Liza had "stood in proxy" for Mary and their other sister. Liza said that while praying for Mary, both Bob and Liza saw a halo of light and a diadem of twinkling stars. "I then believed that what I saw was no dream but God's promise of a new life."

During two hospital confinements, "God enabled me to see the spiritual tumor that had spread into my life—my thoughts, words and actions. The Holy Spirit's touch empowered me to excise the roots of all my harshness and the anger that was slowly killing me. After Bob's and Liza's prayers, the asthma attacks gradually lessened.

"The most unexpected healing," Dr. Mary exclaimed, "is the complete, radiologically confirmed disappearance of the lung tumor. Praise God!" Reflectively, she said, "It was at this

A Crown of Twelve Stars

A great sign appeared in the sky, a woman clothed with the sun, with the moon under her feet, and on her head a crown of twelve stars. Because she was with child, she wailed aloud in pain as she labored to give birth. Then another sign appeared in the sky: it was a huge dragon, flaming red, with seven heads and ten horns; on his heads were seven diadems. His tail swept a third of the stars from the sky and hurled them down to the earth. Then the dragon stood before the woman about to give birth, ready to devour her child when it should be born. She gave birth to a son—a boy destined to shepherd all the nations with an iron rod. Her child was caught up to God and to his throne. The woman herself fled into the desert, where a special place had been prepared for her by God (Rv 12:1-6a).

time that this doctor had to bow down to the Greatest Doctor of all, our Lord Jesus Christ. I offered everything to the Lord, from my stethoscope to my smallest desires and expectations. In return, God gave me complete healing without the use of medical science."

In 1995, Bob Canton and Liza went to the island nation to conduct healing services. In one service, Dr. Mary said, "God gave me the gift of joy which led to reconciliation with another sister. The gift of forgiveness enabled me to love her. For almost six years, we had not spoken in the spirit of love but God healed this relationship."

Dr. Mary hopes that her testimony will focus people's attention "on the goodness of 'Dr. Jesus.'" God still works miracles today!

Other Reported Healings

A man in Nevada testifies: "I was diagnosed three years ago with a tumor in my throat. My doctor had recommended surgery. Since I didn't have adequate insurance coverage, I decided against it.

"I learned about Bob Canton's healing ministry and I called him one evening. He prayed with me over the telephone and I felt heat and tingling sensations in my throat as we prayed. Over the next six weeks, he prayed with me three times. He told me that God was healing me and I should give thanks and praise to the Lord Jesus Christ who is the Divine Healer.

"I recently went to the doctor for more tests. They revealed the tumor had completely disappeared. I immediately praised God the Father, his Son Jesus and the Holy Spirit. I know God loves me very much. Now I constantly turn to him and I aspire to grow in holiness in accordance with his will."

* * *

From Maryland, a woman reports: "In two different prayer services in Maryland, I 'stood in' for my niece and for my brother. Both were addicted to drugs, my niece to heroin. As Bob Canton prayed for her, he had a word of knowledge that she would be completely delivered from her addiction by the power of God.

"At the time of this testimony, my niece has been completely clean for eight months. My brother no longer uses alcohol or drugs and has left a 'heavy metal band' to play and sing for the Lord. He is born again." It's true that nothing is impossible with God if only we believe and trust in him.

* * *

Another reported healing comes from Maryland.

"In August of 1996, I went to a healing service with a friend because she didn't want to go alone. I owed her a favor, so I went because I felt I couldn't say no.

"During the service, Bob Canton asked if there were any deaf or hard of hearing people in the room. I approached him and he touched my ears lightly and asked Jesus in a strong voice to heal nerves. He thanked Jesus all through the prayers.

"When I left the service, I wasn't sure if my hearing was restored or if I was just caught up in the moment. I turned on the car radio. It was blaring! I turned it down low. I heard the words with clarity, which I couldn't do before.

"When I got home, I turned on the television. I could hear what was going on with the volume on medium instead of high. My husband started talking to me and I asked him why he was shouting. He said it was his habit. I told him he didn't have to shout anymore.

"Later that night, in the kitchen, I heard a gentle 'thump, thump, thump.' I was thinking, 'Everyone is asleep. What is that?' Then I noticed Missy, the old family cat, walking across the floor. I was truly amazed. I was actually hearing her footsteps.

"I went back to the company that sold me two sets of hearing aids in five years. They told me, 'The bottom line is, in normal conversation, using both ears, you can hear one hundred percent.'

"I was rather naive about spiritual healing. I had thought Jesus healed the deaf only when he touched them in New Testament times. I had not realized that something that happened two thousand years ago could happen today. The Bible says, 'With God all things are possible.' I have no doubt, now, that this is true.

"As Bob Canton said throughout the service, 'If you are healed, don't thank me. Praise and thank God.'"

* * *

From California comes a report of healed eyesight.

"I had known for about five years that I was going to lose sight in my left eye. On August 20, 1997, I had an appointment with an ophthalmologist for a decision on surgery.

"On August 16, I attended the Mass and healing service at St. Luke's parish in Stockton. After Mass, Bob Canton invited us to come forward for the laying on of hands and healing prayer.

"On August 20, after extensive examinations by my ophthalmologist's technician, I waited in the doctor's office for his prognosis. He went back and forth from the test results on his desk to his notes from my visit in July and then to my eye.

"Three circuits later, he told me that he could find nothing wrong with my left eye! I could tell he was absolutely amazed.

"I am certain that my healing was God's answer to the prayers for me during the healing service. I have told many family and friends of this miraculous cure."

THIRTEEN

"Miracles Do Happen"

+======+

People Who Have Faith Don't Need to See

In her inspiring book, Miracles Do Happen, *Sister Briege McKenna, O.S.C., tells this delightful story experienced while she was giving a retreat to priests in Japan.*

A priest said to her, "Briege, it would be awful easy to believe if I could see a miracle." She told him, "Father, the Lord uses you every morning to perform a miracle."

He said, "I know about the Mass, but you know what I mean. If only I could see somebody healed if they were blind or had bad legs, it would be very easy to believe."

She said, "Oh, do you think it would, Father? I've seen a lot of people healed, but that doesn't make it any easier. I still have to keep praying and many times I find myself thinking, 'Oh, that person's so sick' and wondering if healing is possible."

He said, "Oh, I think I'd be different. I think if I could see a miracle, I would really believe."

About three days later, Father Frank Sullivan (a prominent priest in Roman and Irish circles) was meeting twelve of his Jesuit priests in the room Sr. Briege had been using for ministry. As she walked in, they said, "Oh, Briege, come and pray with us."

She prayed with all of them. Among these Jesuits was an elderly French priest who had very severe gangrene in his leg. The doctor had told him he should have his leg amputated. He asked the doctor to let him make the retreat and then he would go for amputation.

"Blest Are Those Who Have Not Seen ..."

(After Jesus rose from the dead, he appeared to his disciples.) It happened that one of the Twelve, Thomas ... was absent when Jesus came. The other disciples kept telling him: "We have seen the Lord!" His answer was, "I will never believe it without probing the nailprints in his hands, without putting my finger in the nailmarks and my hand into his side."

A week later, the disciples were once more in the room, and this time Thomas was with them. Despite the locked doors, Jesus came and stood before them. "Peace be with you," he said; then, to Thomas: "Take your finger and examine my hands. Put your hand into my side. Do not persist in your unbelief, but believe!" Thomas said in response, "My Lord and my God!" Jesus then said to him, "You became a believer because you saw me. Blest are they who have not seen and have believed" (Jn 20:24-29).

Father Frank asked Sister Briege and all the priests to gather around and pray for healing for the sick priest. The next morning, as Sister Briege was going into breakfast, the French priest came up to her gesticulating and making all kinds of signs, pointing to heaven and to his heart and "just carrying on." Sister Briege doesn't speak French or Japanese, so she couldn't understand what he was trying to say. She just kept looking at him and thought, "This poor man's getting a heart attack or going mad." So she just walked on into breakfast.

The old French priest came running into the room with the legs of this trousers rolled up. He was showing everyone that his leg was perfectly healed.

Three seats down from Sister Briege was her Irish friend who said he could believe if only he could see a miracle.

She told him, "Father, there's your miracle you were talking about the other day."

The Irish priest looked at the healed priest, and then he looked at Sister Briege and he said, "My God, that's hard to believe!"

Then she said to him, "See, Father, it doesn't make it easier to believe."

As Sister Briege puts it, "The moral of this story, I suppose, is that people who have faith don't need to see."

Seeing Is Not Always Believing

Believing in the healing power of prayer is not always easy. Before Sister Briege prayed with me on Halloween Day, 1976,

I found stories about miracles hard to believe. Even when I saw healings, I remained somewhat skeptical. Maybe it's the reporter in me.

In 1975, I attended a retreat in Birmingham, Alabama. The well-known Mother Angelica, who eventually would found Eternal Word Television Network, led the retreat. The retreat closed with a Mass for healing. During the Mass, I was sitting next to a woman in her seventies who had lived all her life with a huge birthmark and warts on her face. In addition, she had a large tumor bulging in her left cheek and, as I learned later, five other tumors in her body. She was scheduled for surgery the following Tuesday to remove the tumors.

After Communion, as Mother Angelica prayed for God to heal those who needed healing, I watched in amazement as the woman's facial tumor disappeared before my eyes. Later, I learned that when she reported for surgery the doctors took more x-rays. All the tumors were gone. And more! The birthmark and warts vanished from her face!

And still, I harbored doubts about God's love until that day when Sister Briege prayed for me.

FOURTEEN

A Marriage Is Healed Through Continual Prayer

In Miracles Do Happen, *Sister Briege recounts a beautiful story about a man who found the power to forgive, and with it, a new and deeper relationship with his wife.*

Some time ago, when I was giving a couple's retreat, a gentleman came to me. He was terribly distraught because his marriage was in great difficulty. He and his wife were becoming involved in many different things and couldn't relate to each other. To further complicate the situation, he had evidence that his wife had been unfaithful. He had gone to a marriage counselor who told him to give her an ultimatum and if that didn't work, to get a divorce.

The man said it shattered him because he just couldn't

accept divorce as an answer to his problem. He didn't know what to do.

I brought him into the church before the tabernacle. The Lord gave me a word for him: that it would get worse, but it would get better. This wasn't a very consoling word for me to give this poor man.

I told him that this would be a test of his faith, that sometimes we have to persist in prayer and in interceding for someone. I explained that when we intercede for others, God can work in our lives, too, and we can come to believe that miracles do happen. I told him that an increase in faith was one benefit of persevering prayer.

After this, he would travel long distances or phone me to have me pray with him. All I would ever do was say to him, "Let's pray and don't give up."

He'd say to me, "I love my wife." He felt in his heart that the Lord did not want him to walk out of his wife's life, that their marriage was blessed by the Church, that it was a sacrament. But at the same time, all of his counselors were saying, "I'd leave her."

Yet each time he spoke with me, I'd encourage him not to give up. I'd remind him that Jesus said that nothing is impossible for the man who believes.

I sympathized with him. "It's a very difficult thing to identify with someone who keeps on rejecting you, but you identify with Jesus. Even to this day, Jesus loves us and we reject him all the time. He doesn't stop loving us. If you set out to heal your own marriage, you couldn't do it. But you can ask Jesus to give you supernatural strength. This won't take away the suffering and the pain of rejection, but you will have the strength to persevere."

One day he phoned me and said, "Sister Briege, I want to thank you. God answered our prayer." He then related to me a beautiful spiritual experience that he and his wife had had. One evening, the two of them had sensed God's transforming presence as they were preparing for bed.

The Power of Prayer

(Jesus said:) "Ask, and you will receive. Seek, and you will find. Knock, and it will be opened to you. For the one who asks, receives. The one who seeks, finds. The one who knocks, enters. Would one of you hand his son a stone when he asks for a loaf, or a poisonous snake when he asks for a fish? If you, with all your sins, know how to give your children what is good, how much more will your heavenly Father give good things to anyone who asks him!" (Mt 7:7-10).

He had not had relations with his wife for some time because the knowledge of her unfaithfulness was a barrier to his expression of love. But when they were in bed that night, the Lord enveloped the two of them in his love and he recreated in them the love they had had when they were first married. He transformed them. Not only did he renew their marriage, but he gave them gifts of the Holy Spirit.

The man said he wanted to come to see me. I happened to be in the city where he lived, so I told him to come over. When he came to see me, he said, "Sister Briege, I hope this will not be an insult to you, but you were a great signpost to Jesus. Many days when I was going to my work, I felt like just going to a divorce court, thinking, 'Why should I live through this?' But every time I talked to you, you turned me around by pointing to Jesus. You didn't take me there, but you sure told me what Jesus could do. That's what a signpost does—it doesn't take you where you want to go, but it points out the direction to go.

"I learned two lessons from all this," he said. "First, I can never take my marriage for granted. I loved my wife, but I never really told her. Second, I must never underestimate the power of prayer and the supernatural strength that comes through it."

God still heals today!

FIFTEEN

They Were Blind, But Now They See

✛━━✛

Agnes Mac is married and has four children. She is a pediatrician. Her husband, Robert, is a pharmacist. They live in Warsaw, Poland.

Agnes says she "met Jesus" when she was thirteen years old through a movement called Light and Life. For the next seventeen years, she had a good relationship with her Lord.

However, her faith was to be tested. She developed a problem with her sight. The retina of one eye was badly formed, causing vision problems. While in the hospital for corrective surgery, Agnes prayed for healing. The surgery was unsuccessful, and the surgeon told her she would never be healed.

In 1995, Agnes went to a meeting at which Ralph Martin was speaking and ministering. Ralph is known worldwide for his healing and teaching ministry and is the founder and pres-

---

The Second Touch ...

When they arrived at Bethsaida, some people brought him a blind man and begged him to touch him. Jesus took the blind man's hand and led him outside the village. Putting spittle on his eyes he laid his hands on him and asked, "Can you see anything?" The man opened his eyes and said, "I can see people but they look like walking trees!" Then a second time Jesus laid hands on his eyes, and he saw perfectly; his sight was restored and he could see everything clearly (Mk 8:22-25).

---

ident of Renewal Ministries in Ann Arbor, Michigan.

During the prayer meeting, someone received a word of knowledge that a person present at the gathering had an eye problem. Agnes said that she knew in her heart that she was the one about whom they were speaking.

"Some men prayed over me and when the meeting ended Ralph prayed over me again. I felt nothing, except that I took some deep breaths. Those around me noticed rapid eye movement. I had no further feelings that could be a sign of a healing.

"Ralph said I should continue to pray to the Holy Spirit for healing," Agnes said. "After three weeks, I recovered my sight. My sight was good and still is after all this time."

This doctor, wife and mother says she also thanks God for an internal healing. While in the hospital, when she was praying so hard for complete healing, and when that healing did not occur, she didn't feel the Lord was with her. "I longed for

Jesus, but I didn't feel his presence."

However, "after Ralph prayed, something happened," said Agnes. "I felt the presence of the Holy Spirit in my heart. My spiritual life was changed. I began to worship God and to be thankful. I have a joy in my heart, a laughter that drives away fear. There is no fear."

This was the beginning of another kind of healing as well. "With this new spiritual healing in my heart, there began a healing and strengthening in my relationships with my husband and my children. My husband and I grew closer and our love deepened. My love for my children grew even stronger."

At the time of her healing, Agnes and Robert had three children. She became pregnant with their fourth child but was told that natural delivery was out of the question. The physical strain and pressure would be too much for her eye. "But I recognized in my heart that God was giving me the gift of a natural birth," said Agnes.

There was a natural birth.

Two Healings in Hungary

Dennis Donahue, from Temecula, California, has multiple sclerosis. He occasionally experiences blindness and has had to go on disability. However, his own problems do not keep Dennis from reaching out to other people.

Renewal Ministries was holding a rally in Hungary. Besides Dennis, the team included Ralph Martin and Ann Shields, internationally known for her ministry in teaching and healing. During this mission, Dennis prayed with two different blind people and they were healed. The accounts of these two healings appeared in an issue of the Renewal Ministries newsletter.

Ralph had just finished his talk on a personal relationship with Jesus Christ, and he invited people to come up to pray for the grace to turn to Christ. Two ladies approached Dennis and Vera, his interpreter. One was helping the other, who seemed to be blind.

The first lady said her friend had been born blind and would like prayer for healing. Dennis told them to come back for prayer after the next talk, but the blind woman said she also wanted a deeper relationship with Jesus. She asked Dennis to pray for healing of her blindness at the same time.

Dennis and Vera prayed for her and the woman rested in the Spirit. He said, "I never in my life saw so many tears flow from a person's eyes. She fell with her arms straight up in the air and I felt she was being healed."

Ann Shields' talk was scheduled to start in five minutes, so Dennis quickly ran downstairs to the team room for a drink of water. When he got back, the woman with whom he had prayed was standing, looking around. "I just prayed for you," he told her. "She told me her eyes were healed along with her feet, which were also handicapped. She was crying, saying that she and her friend were waiting there to meet a priest to verify a miracle!"

After Ann Shields' talk, a grandmother brought her granddaughter to Dennis for prayer. He spoke to the grandmother through Vera, his interpreter, and learned that the child had been blind since birth.

"She had glasses on," Dennis explains, "but they were being used to cover the deformity of her eyelids. Vera and I prayed for her and bound the spirit of blindness." They continued to pray for the girl but it was now time for another talk. "We prayed with her until the last minute."

Dennis then made his way to his seat. "As I approached where Vera and I were sitting, I looked up at the stage and saw the grandmother and the little girl up there. The girl was standing with her back to the crowd and the grandmother was sitting and sobbing. I approached the stage and the grandmother saw me and pointed me out to the little girl.

"She turned around and looked into my eyes. Her face was very beautiful. I saw Jesus in her restored eyes. She came running to me and hugged me gently. I felt as though I was being hugged by Jesus and his great mercy. We all sobbed deeply and joyfully, and the girl and her grandmother gave testimony of the miracle which was verified by a priest who knew the family."

SIXTEEN

God Can Do Two Healings at Once

Franciscan Father Michael Scanlan is chancellor of the Franciscan University of Steubenville, a speaker at FIRE rallies and the author of several books and pamphlets.

Father Michael shares two stories with us. The first comes from his book Let the Fire Fall *and shows God's power made manifest in weakness. The second describes the healing of his relationship with his stepfather.*

Father Michael has graciously given me permission to reprint the stories here.

Revelation often hits me when I am ill. It probably has something to do with being in a position where I *know* that I am weak and need the Lord, something I tend to forget when I am well.

This revelation happened one frigid January afternoon in

1971. I had returned to the Franciscan seminary from a conference in Ann Arbor, Michigan. Hong Kong flu had swept through the Ann Arbor assembly like one of the plagues of Egypt. Most of the speakers at the conference, including speakers who had led healing workshops, had been struck down. I had a particularly severe case. I had actually checked into the hospital in Ann Arbor because I was showing signs of malaria, apparently contracted five months earlier in the Amazon. After a few more days of rest in Michigan, I managed to get on a plane and returned home, still very ill.

About an hour after I got home, I was lying face down on my bed, trying to get up enough strength to change into my pajamas, when I heard a knock on my door. It was a seminarian. He jumped into the room on one foot.

"Father Mike, my foot's broken," he said as he slumped into a chair. "I'm sure of it. I was playing volleyball. I went up for a block, came down on the side of my foot, and I heard it crack."

I looked at him with half-closed eyes. Did he want my permission to go to the hospital? I had never been so sick in my life. I couldn't move. I felt bad for him, but I felt worse for myself.

"Could you pray with me, Father?" he asked.

Was he kidding? Some people around the seminary made little jokes about the charismatic revival that had been going on. But this young man wasn't one of them. I decided that he was serious. He really wanted the deathly ill rector to pray for his foot.

"I can't get up, Bill," I said. "Bring your foot over here."

He dragged his chair across the floor and put his foot in my face. I raised my arm, and put it on his swollen foot.

"Jesus, please heal Bill's foot," I croaked. That was all I could say or do.

Bill said, "look," and about thirty seconds later he was bounding around the room. "It's healed. My foot's healed. Father, you healed my foot." He ran out of the room and down the corridor yelling, "Come look at this, brothers, my foot was broken, but Father Mike healed it."

A Thorn in My Side ...

As to the extraordinary revelations, in order that I might not become conceited I was given a thorn in the flesh, an angel of Satan to beat me and keep me from getting proud. Three times I begged the Lord that this might leave me. He said to me, "My grace is enough for you, for in weakness power reaches perfection." And so I willingly boast of my weaknesses instead, that the power of Christ may rest upon me (2 Cor 12:7b-9).

I lay there in bodily misery but in spiritual fervor. "*I* didn't heal him, Lord, but you did," I said. "Why did it work so simply?"

I reflected. Of course, the Lord healed Bill because he loved him, but I thought there was a message for me in that healing, too. I had been struggling to overcome my pride and vanity for many years. Perhaps the Lord wanted to work through me at a time when there was no doubt that *he* was the one who was acting.

But there was more. Later, when I had recovered a little, I reached for my Bible and prayed for a passage. My hand fell on Acts 4:29 (RSV). The passage described the great thanksgiving of the Jerusalem church after the authorities released Peter and John. In this time of persecution and great trial, the people prayed: "Lord, look upon their threats, and grant to thy servants to speak thy word with all boldness, while thou stretchest out thy hand to heal, and signs and wonders are performed through the name of thy holy servant Jesus."

This is, I realized, a time of visitation. Our time is an era of accelerating evil and great pressure on the Church. It is also a time when God is working with great power, when his graces are available in an abundance and with a kind of public exposure that is without precedent.

The story of my involvement in the healing ministry is the story of learning how healing both embodies and points toward the large thing God is doing among us. It is a story of God's great, merciful love and my weakness.

He Helped His Stepfather Into the Church

One of the clear moments of healing in my life had to do with a healing of the heart concerning my mother's husband. My father and mother separated when I was three years old, and a few years later, they divorced. Shortly after that, my father moved to Mexico, and I would see him once every two or three years. When I was in the ninth grade, my mother married a man named Bill.

Bill was a very good provider and companion for my mother. He was very difficult to live with because he had little understanding of children, never having had any of his own. Also, he was strongly anti-Catholic and verbally violent about it. He feared that I might become a priest and he spent time planning and plotting how to move me from a Catholic environment.

Part of the motivation that Bill had to be anti-Catholic was the fact that since my mother had not received an annulment from her previous marriage, the Church did not recognize her marriage to Bill and she was not able to receive the sacraments.

Bill was very exacting about the chores I had to complete and would show great disgust if in any way I was deficient in my chores, in the way I dressed or in the way I communicated with my friends. Because of this, I closed my heart to him and developed a hardened heart. Internally, I decided I would live independently of him and not let him bother me. I told my mother that I was no longer afraid of him and that I could live my life alongside of him.

Many years passed. While he was proud of my achievements—he would brag about me to others—he would never affirm me directly. At this point I expected nothing, so I was not disappointed. It was many years before I learned that he was too bound up inside to express love and appreciation directly.

I graduated from Harvard law school and Bill seemed to be warming up in acknowledging some of my accomplishments. He remained suspicious about the Catholic things I was doing.

After taking the New York Bar Exam, I signed up with a Wall Street law firm but was then called into active duty in the Air Force. Bill seemed reasonably proud of the position I held as Staff Judge Advocate at Andrews Air Force Base, near Washington, D.C. This quickly changed when I announced fourteen months later that I was going to leave the Air Force and join the Franciscan order to study for the priesthood. He expressed in every way his rejection of me. He said that since my mother had her heart set on my being a lawyer and giving her grandchildren, I was ruining my mother's life.

I joined the Franciscans, and after a visit by my mother and Bill there was a great change in my mother's view of my life and she was supportive. Bill became very quiet and didn't express any negative thoughts. He did attempt on my visit home to get me involved with women as a last effort to change my vocational direction.

It was almost two years later, after I had taken simple vows in the Franciscan way of life, that Bill unexpectedly fell ill and was taken to the hospital. He had always been very proud of his perfect health and looked down on any of us who had allergies or colds or other physical weaknesses.

At this time he wrote me, asking why God would put him in the hospital. I took this opening to propose to him that it was so that God could get his attention and bring him to a clear commitment in life as well as to a life in the Church. He accepted this in a passive way and over the next year, he began to get close to a Franciscan priest from New York City. This led to a brother-sister relationship between my mother and Bill, by which my mother could go back to the sacraments and Bill could come much closer to the Catholic Church.

The following year, my mother died unexpectedly. Following her death, it seemed that Bill accepted and took on more of her values in life. At the time of her death, my mother was so very grateful for the grace of living once again a full Catholic life. Her gratitude led her to spend mornings in service to the poor. Every day she went to Mass and adoration of the Blessed Sacrament. She was in church from noon to five o'clock. She experienced mystical graces before she died and was truly a beautiful and holy woman.

In the years following her death, the one thing that kept Bill and me together was a common love for my mother. I went on in my Franciscan way of life and was ordained a priest. I served as dean of the College of Steubenville and the rector-president of St. Francis Major Seminary.

While in the seminary, I became active in charismatic prayer meetings. At one of the prayer meetings, I heard teachings and witnesses about how much God loves us and wants to heal past hurts in our lives. When the meeting was over, I asked a couple of close friends to pray with me so my heart could be healed regarding my relationship with Bill. As they prayed, I could feel the hardness of my heart breaking away. It was a cracking sensation in which many of the negative feelings buried there over the years were now brought forth. This was followed by tears and then by an experience of God's love for me and for Bill. I suddenly knew that I could love him and care for him. This was entirely new.

In subsequent years, I helped Bill become a Catholic. I regularly visited him. I was the only one with him during his dying days, and he told me that he was so deeply grateful that I had loved him and been faithful to the end when everyone else had disappeared from his life. I knew a great peace at Bill's funeral. I knew that I had loved him with the Lord's love and that the Lord's love had brought him into the Church and home to God. I knew that it was God's free gift of merciful love that had changed my heart. I can still see Bill in those very last days, with medals and scapulars around his neck and a book of devotional prayer near his bedside. He was gentle. He was awaiting and accepting Sister Death.

I thank God for his healing, grace and love. People who knew us were absolutely amazed that we became so close in the later years. They couldn't understand how it happened when it had been so clear to all the world that there was seemingly a permanent chasm between us.

God provided the bridge.

SEVENTEEN

A Surgeon Makes a Surprising Discovery

June and Jack are married and, at the time of this healing, lived in a large midwestern city. Their dream of raising a family almost died when June was diagnosed with a life-threatening tumor.

June, a physically active woman, had been having backaches for a couple of years but her doctor could find nothing seriously wrong. Then, in 1982, when she was thirty years old, the pain escalated sharply over the Thanksgiving holiday. The day before Thanksgiving, she left work with severe back pain. Her doctor told her to take it easy and report to the hospital on Monday for tests.

Over the weekend, June took a hot bath to help relieve the pain but when the time came to get out of the tub, she couldn't. Jack helped her get out and get dressed but June decided that, in spite of the pain, she would wait until Monday to consult the doctor. By Sunday, however, she couldn't walk and she went to the hospital Sunday evening.

On Monday morning, the doctor decided to operate. Surgery revealed a tumor wrapped around her spinal cord and apparently growing within her spinal column. The doctor removed some of the tumor and tests revealed that although it was not cancerous, it was growing and was life-threatening. As it grew upward, it would eventually damage the nerves that controlled breathing, and death could follow. The doctor had recently lost a patient with this same condition. Even if the disease were not fatal, June would be paralyzed from the waist down and could never have children.

The doctor offered only one solution. He suggested that June find a doctor who would agree to remove the tumor and sever the spinal cord. The tumor would be gone and June would be paralyzed, but she would live.

At about this time, a priest from Brooklyn with a healing ministry happened to be in the area. The priest was a friend of June's uncle, so he came to visit her. They talked for awhile and then the priest asked her about her family. June told him about Jack and her parents but he said, "No, I mean, do you have any children?" June told him no, that she and Jack had only been married about a year.

The priest looked at her intently and said, "You will." Then he prayed with June and left, and she didn't give the incident much more thought.

June's large extended family prayed for her, and Jack's uncle, a priest, invited family and friends to a Mass to pray for spiritual help. At that Mass was a cousin who knew a neurosurgeon from Ireland now teaching at a local university. June went to see him and he recommended a different approach. He wanted to go in, expand the spinal column and treat the tumor with radiation. He had to expand the column because radiation makes the spinal cord swell, and without space to expand, the spinal fluid would be cut off.

June and Jack agreed to give radiation a try but they—and the doctor—were in for a surprise. When the surgeon made the incision, the tumor just popped away from the spinal cord and he was able to remove all of it. The surgeon later said that there was only about one chance in one hundred that this would happen.

This was a life-altering experience for June and Jack and they are convinced that the prayers of family and friends led them to the right doctor. They had no reason to know him nor had they ever heard of radiation therapy for this situation.

After surgery, June was still paralyzed from the waist down due to trauma to the spinal cord, but she didn't need radiation or chemotherapy. She entered an area rehabilitation center run by a religious order and has since recovered almost all of her mobility. Not only is she very active and holding down a job, but she is also the mother of six children!

Having children took courage. June was using two canes—the kind with four-pronged pedestals—when she became pregnant with her first child in 1984. Two years later, she had graduated to two simple canes when her twin girls were born. Subsequently, she gradually gave up all use of a cane and has since had three more children, two boys and a girl.

June beams when she talks about the power of prayer. And she has a great sense of humor. After listing the arrival of all her children, she says that now she is praying for menopause.

EIGHTEEN

A Busy Saint and God's Mercy

+≈+

Praying to and with the saints has long been a Catholic tradition. It's still in style and it still works, even if the saint is not a full-blown, canonized one.

Sister Faustina Kowalska, a Polish nun born in 1905, is one of these powerful intercessors. She joined the Sisters of Our Lady of Mercy and died of tuberculosis in 1938.

In the 1930s, Sister Faustina received a message from the Lord about his divine mercy. According to the booklet, "The Divine Mercy, Message and Devotion," she was asked to become "the apostle and secretary of God's mercy, a model of how to be merciful to others, and an instrument for reemphasizing God's plan of mercy for the world."

Her entire life was to be a sacrifice. She was to be "a doer of mercy" and bring joy and peace to others. By "writing about God's mercy, she was to encourage others to trust in him and thus prepare the world for his coming again."

Blessed Faustina's intercession led to Maureen Digan's miraculous healing in 1981. This healing was accepted in Rome, in 1993, as one of the miracles necessary to move Sister Faustina up the ladder toward canonization.

Father Ron Pytel is another person who has benefitted miraculously through the intercession of Blessed Faustina. He had a bad heart, underwent surgery and experienced an unprecedented healing. His healing is being considered in the cause of canonization of Blessed Faustina.

The ABC's of Mercy

Sister Faustina's devotion is beautifully capsuled in this way:

Ask for his mercy. "Ask and it will be given you ... for everyone who asks receives" (Mt 7:7,8, RSV).

Be merciful. "A new commandment I give you.... As I have loved you, so you must love one another" (Jn 13:34, NIV). "Be merciful even as your Father is merciful" (Lk 6:36, RSV).

Completely trust. "I am love and mercy itself.... Let no soul fear to draw near to me, even though its sins be as scarlet."

(From Blessed Faustina's writings about her messages from God.)

In Maureen Digan's Own Words

I enjoyed a normal, healthy and happy life until I turned fifteen. Then I came down with lymphedema, a serious disease that causes swelling of the legs.

Within the next ten years, I had more than fifty operations. Numerous stays in the hospital varied in duration, from as brief as a week to as long as a year. Family and visitors would say, "Pray and trust in God; he is good." I thought, "You must be

---

The Importance and Intercession of Saints

"By canonizing some of the faithful, i.e., by solemnly proclaiming that they practiced heroic virtue and lived in fidelity to God's grace, the Church recognizes the power of the spirit of holiness within her and sustains the hope of believers by proposing the saints to them as models and intercessors" *(Catechism of the Catholic Church,* No. 828).

"The witnesses who have preceded us into the kingdom, especially those whom the Church recognizes as saints, share in the living tradition of prayer by the example of their lives, the transmission of their writings and their prayers today. They contemplate God, praise him and constantly care for those whom they have left on earth. When they entered into the joy of their Master, they were 'put in charge of many things' (cf. Mt 25:21). Their intercession is their most exalted service to God's plan. We can and should ask them to intercede for us and for the whole world" *(Catechism of the Catholic Church,* No. 2683).

kidding. Faith and trust? In the One who keeps knocking me down? Thanks, but no thanks! Not me. I can do it by myself."

At times I did pray a little, but only with my lips, not in my heart. "Super Maureen" didn't need any help, especially spiritual help. I cried when I was alone, but smiled for friends and medical staff so no one would know how I really felt.

I built a wall around myself, never realizing that my illness could bring me closer to the Lord. I was too busy living in my own world of pain.

I was dating Bob at the time. He was in the Marines and would often drive eighteen hours to sit and visit with me in the hospital. I was so angry with everyone and so mixed up that sometimes I would be glad to see him and other times I wouldn't even act human to him. I felt his feelings for me must have been out of sympathy, not love. If God doesn't love me, how could this cute Marine love me? So, finally, I broke up with Bob and then blamed it on God. Everything was God's fault, not Maureen's fault.

I found any and every reason not to go to Mass or confession. I didn't need confession. I hadn't done anything wrong. It was God who was wrong, not me. So I used my illness for what I thought was my advantage: "Oh, I'm too sick to go to Mass. I'm in too much pain." No wonder I was so unhappy!

As my condition worsened, the operations became more extreme. Spinal surgery, which the doctors had hoped would save my right leg, left me paralyzed for two years. Then my leg had to be amputated anyway, first above the knee, and then, six months later, all the way to the hip. The amputations were very difficult, especially because I could not or would not turn to God for comfort and strength.

I began to feel safe in the hospital. I could hide there. I

> In my heart I heard Sister Faustina say, "Ask for my help and I will help you."

didn't have to face the real world and let people know just how I was feeling. It was a big struggle. I knew in my heart I should turn to God, but I wouldn't let myself. "No," I told myself, "I won't do that. I can do it alone. 'Super Maureen' doesn't need any help from God."

I was finally discharged from the hospital and later got a job there. At this time, Bob reentered my life and I realized that this was true love, not sympathy. On my birthday, Bob asked me if I would marry him, and I did the first right thing I had done in years by saying, "Yes."

But the problems continued. Four months after our marriage, I had a miscarriage. We were told our chances of ever having a child were slim. "OK, God, another punishment. Pain medication? Sure, I'll take it. Anything that will help me forget my physical and mental pain."

God bless Bob! I don't know how he did it. He stayed so faithful and never complained. But I *do* know how he did it. It was his strong faith, his trust in God.

After two years I became pregnant again, and I thought, "Maybe God can be good to me." Nine months later, our little darling Bobby was born, brain damaged. At twenty-one months, Bobby had his first grand mal seizure. He lost his ability to walk and talk and was in and out of hospitals constantly.

On his sixth birthday, Bobby was admitted to the hospital weighing thirty-five pounds, and discharged five-and-a-half months later weighing eighteen pounds and being fed through a tube.

I roomed in with Bobby at the hospital for that whole time and never once went home, even to cook a meal for my hard-working husband. But, as always, Bob never complained. It must have been difficult for him to go to work each day with Bobby so sick.

The doctors suggested that we put Bobby in an institution, but we wanted him home with us. So home we went.

Meanwhile, my lymphedema was getting worse and I was hospitalized seven times myself that year. I started having seizures due to stress and depression and I was put on a program of very strong pain medications, antidepressants and seizure medications.

One evening Bob went to see the first movie made about Divine Mercy and Sister Faustina, and he became convinced of the truth of the Mercy message. He tried to share this with me, but I wouldn't listen. I wasn't interested.

He didn't push me. He just sat back and prayed, and he received what he later called a "collect call" from God to take his family to the tomb of Sister Faustina in Poland. He contacted Father Seraphim Michalenko, MIC, the vice postulator of Sister Faustina's beatification cause, and he obtained permission to accompany us on the trip.

I didn't want to go so far from home with a priest I was then afraid of and a husband I thought was turning into a religious fanatic. But I finally realized that, for the sake of my marriage, I should stop complaining and go.

The doctor agreed to discharge me from the hospital, because he was convinced I would lose my remaining leg soon, and it would be much harder for me to travel after that.

On March 23, 1981, on Bobby's birthday, we arrived in Poland. On March 28, I made the first good confession I had made since I was very young. Afterward, I felt a closeness to the Lord and to Sister Faustina, but I was afraid to let myself get too close.

That night, at the tomb of Sister Faustina, we concluded a novena of prayers, reciting the Chaplet of Divine Mercy and another prayer asking for a healing for Bobby and me through her intercession. In my heart I heard Sister Faustina say, "Ask for my help and I will help you." Still in my bad attitude, I felt myself respond, "OK, Faustina, you brought me this far from home, now do something!"

Suddenly the pain left me. I didn't believe in miracles, so I was convinced I was having a nervous breakdown. The next day I noticed that the swelling was gone. I had to stuff my shoe with tissue so my shoe wouldn't fall off and so people wouldn't notice that the swelling was all gone.

It was three or four days later before I was finally able to accept that I really had received a blessed gift of healing from God.

I also became aware of a new feeling of closeness to God and a strange sense that I, myself, was a new person. I wasn't so much "Super Maureen" any longer but was now able to rely on God and trust in his merciful love.

Lymphedema is a disease that does not respond to medication and does not go into remission. But I have seen five independent doctors, all of whom concur that I have been 100 percent healed. My friends and members of my family were called in as witnesses by officials from the Boston Archdiocese and questioned about what they knew about me and my healing.

The testimony and documents gathered in Boston were then sent to the investigating tribunal in Poland where the healing had taken place.

In 1986, the process concerning the healing was completed in Poland, and the official documents were sent to Rome and presented to the Sacred Congregation for the Causes of Saints.

(The Congregation did accept the miracle and it was used in the beatification of Sister Faustina.)

Bobby's vocation in life was different. He received a dramatic but incomplete healing that allowed him to live an almost normal life for three-and-a-half wonderful years. He was off all medication, learned to ride a bike and won gold and silver medals in the Special Olympics. Then his condition worsened, and he went to the Lord in May of 1991.

Father Seraphim and The Divine Mercy Shrine rector, Father Joe DiCine, both of whom had known Bobby since he was a little boy, were with us the day Bobby died. Thanks to these two priests, Bobby was never afraid to meet the Lord.

On Mother's Day, Bobby put his thin little arms around my neck and said, "Mom, I have something to tell you. God will send his Son Jesus to take me to heaven soon. Don't be afraid or sad." Then he called his dad in and told him the same thing.

There is a great deal of suffering involved, but to be a parent to a handicapped child is such a blessing, such a gift from God! We learned so much from Bobby, and we could never measure the love he radiated to all he met.

Life is so different when you are close to the Lord! We are so grateful to God for my healing and for the time he gave us with Bobby. And we understand that, out of our great loss, God has come and will continue to come.

It is still not easy. I have to work every day at staying close to the Lord, and Father Joe is continuing to minister to Bob and me and help us in our walk with God.

I hope that this sharing of our life journey will be a source of consolation and hope for others, especially for those in painful circumstances. Please don't get as low as I did before you turn to the Lord. He is always there for us. No sin—not even trying to avoid him in our lives—is too great for him to forgive.

As for confession, I feel that the greatest miracles take place there. It is there that we find peace, love, joy and forgiveness.

Father Ron Pytel: "His Heart Touched Mine"

They say it helps to have friends in high places. And Father Ron Pytel has learned he definitely has friends he can count on.

When Father Ron had a serious heart ailment two years ago, his friends prayed. Another friend, Blessed Faustina Kowalska, interceded. And the answer to those prayers may be recognized as the miracle that raises Blessed Faustina to sainthood.

Yet the forty-nine-year-old pastor of Holy Rosary Parish in Baltimore, Maryland is quick to point out that Jesus healed him. "I know in my heart that Blessed Faustina put in a word with Jesus, and his heart touched mine. It's as simple as that," he says.

The first thing you notice about Father Ron when you meet him is that he is a man completely at peace. "I've had a peace that has been with me through everything that has taken place," he explains. "I've also been blessed with a calmness, a gentleness. I think it's made me more open to the struggles of other people."

And Father Ron has certainly had his own struggles. They began in 1995 when he found himself out of breath after walking up a flight of stairs. Father Ron had developed bronchitis but he knew something else was wrong. His friend, Father Larry Gesy, referred him to Dr. Nicholas Fortuin, a world-renowned cardiologist at Johns Hopkins Hospital in Baltimore.

Upon examination, the doctor discovered that Father Ron's aortic valve, was blocked by a buildup of calcium. As a result, the left ventricle of the heart had been badly damaged. He explains it like this: When you blow up a new balloon, it stretches and will never return to its original shape. That's what had happened to the left ventricle of his heart.

In June 1995, Father Ron had surgery to replace the valve with an artificial one, but the damage to his heart was another problem. When he went for his first regular checkup two months later, the prognosis was not good. "Dr. Fortuin didn't say much to me," Father Ron says. "He told my friend, Father Larry, the news and asked him to break it to me gently. Basically, he said my heart would never be normal. He didn't even think I would be able to resume my regular pastoral duties."

But God wasn't quite done with Father Ron Pytel. Later that summer, he was supposed to lead a group of Baltimore pilgrims to Poland, making stops at places where Blessed Faustina had lived and worked. (His parish houses the Archdiocesan Shrine of The Divine Mercy.) But Father Ron was not well enough to go.

At Blessed Faustina's tomb, Holy Rosary Parishioner Dorothy Olszewski prayed for a miracle for Father Ron. The entire group prayed for him daily.

On October 5, Blessed Faustina's feast day, after all-day devotions at Holy Rosary, Father Ron went forward at a special healing service. "Blessed Faustina was invoked. I venerated the relic and I collapsed on the floor. I couldn't move. I was conscious, but I felt as though I was paralyzed," he said.

After fifteen minutes, Father Ron recalls, one of the women

from the healing ministry told him, "Friends in high places are keeping you there. You can get up now."

Father Ron was unprepared for the news that Dr. Fortuin had for him after his next checkup. After a battery of tests, Father Ron says the cardiologist put his elbows on his desk and said, "Someone has intervened for you. Your heart is normal. I'll see you in a year."

"I don't even remember getting on the elevator that day," Father Ron says. "I called Father Larry and told him the news. He was stunned. Then he said, 'Well, we got the miracle we prayed for.'"

The healing of Father Ron's heart in itself is not miraculous. In one percent of cases in which a person's heart is severely damaged, there is such recovery. But in those cases, the healing takes place over a two or three year period! Father Ron's healing occurred within a three month period, less than six months after surgery.

Soon after being given a clean bill of health in November 1995, Father Ron contacted Father Seraphim Michalenko, MIC, vice-postulator for Blessed Faustina's canonization cause. The Marian priest from Stockbridge had proved instrumental in securing the documentation that was needed for Maureen Digan's miracle that led to Sister Faustina's beatification.

A year later, in November 1996, a full canonical inquiry was held by the Archdiocese of Baltimore. In mid-December, Fr. Seraphim and Fr. Ron delivered depositions, medical records and sworn testimonies to the Congregation for the Cause of

Saints in Rome. The case was opened in January 1997 for the healing as the miracle needed for Blessed Faustina's canonization.

As a priest with a drive to promote the devotion, Father Ron is delighted that his healing has touched off an explosion of interest in Divine Mercy.

And the peace and compassion he has been blessed with have helped him minister that mercy to those who are in need. He particularly stresses the sacraments of Eucharist and Reconciliation in ministry.

"I want people to realize that the source of healing is from our Lord in the Blessed Sacrament," he explains. "It's the sacramental life of the Church that is the source of Jesus' healing. That's Faustina's whole message."

Love, Friendship and Faith Brought Carolyn Home

⊹⊱━━⊰⊹

The phone rang twice before Carolyn answered in a lively, clear voice. And that is something because Carolyn shouldn't be alive today. The aneurysm in her brain was supposed to have killed her in January 1989.

However, after six months in a hospital bed, Carolyn did go home and love, friendship and faith, she said, are the reasons why.

"Without the love and support it would have been easy to just lie down and die," the then forty-four-year-old said in an interview in late 1989. "When you're going through something like this, all you can do is pray, pray, pray, and hold onto each other for dear life."

"You're looking at a miracle; she's the miracle," said her husband, Johnny, holding Carolyn's hand. "I remember rushing her to the hospital at five in the morning. I didn't even have on a shirt or shoes," he said, recalling the day she woke him up complaining of a terrible headache.

"I thought she was going to die in my arms."

For the next thirty-two days, Carolyn was in a coma. A "flicker of an eyebrow" and "the wiggle of a toe" were the only signs of life.

"In the beginning the doctor told me there was a good chance she wasn't going to make it," Johnny said. "He told me to prepare myself for the worst."

Parishioners from St. Margaret Mary Church in Winter Park, Florida—the family's parish for nearly thirty years—rallied to support Johnny, Carolyn and their four children. The community raised $80,000 to help pay for medical costs that soared to more than $250,000 (it was all paid off in 1989). The family had no health insurance.

Johnny joyfully explains: "We were down to nothing. Carolyn had a travel agency, but we had to close that. I kept my hair styling business. We kept the house, but we sold one of the cars. We had to cash in all our savings, all the IRAs. We were down to nothing, but it's all come back tenfold!"

When Carolyn was in the hospital, members of Johnny's prayer group took turns keeping him company at the hospital, at first around the clock, then early morning to after midnight. Thousands of people—parishioners, friends and business associates—prayed for Carolyn's recovery.

"I spent every hour I was awake praying. I didn't even drive the first couple of months. Someone was always there to pick me up in the morning and bring me home at night," Johnny said.

At his wife's bedside, Johnny talked and sang to Carolyn while she was in the coma. Sometimes he'd sing religious songs, sometimes he would make up words as he went along. Other times he'd ask her to heal herself, or tell her that the morning sun—shining on her bed through the hospital window—would make her well again.

"Emotionally there were a lot of ups and downs," Johnny said. "Every time she took a turn for the worse it would tear my heart out. No way I would have made it through this thing without faith."

Doctors removed the aneurysm, but Carolyn suffered a stroke while in the hospital. In late 1989, she walked six steps across her bedroom with a walker, her first steps in nine months. A wheelchair became her only way to move around the house, but Carolyn exercised every day in the family's back-yard pool. Johnny would work only in the afternoon so he could coach her in the pool.

"We don't know yet how far she's going to come. We don't know if she'll ever walk again," Johnny said in the 1989 inter-view. Her legs had atrophied but she did walk again. It took a year and a half for Johnny to help her move up from the wheel-chair to crutches, to a walker and a cane. Today, Carolyn uses that cane only when she has a long distance to go.

Despite the burden that Carolyn's illness delivered, the fam-ily insisted that it was not a tragedy; in a way it was a good thing. So many people prayed for them "and today," Johnny said, "Carolyn is a living testimony to God's love and healing power. People she doesn't even know come up to her and hug her. The other day, we met a friend from the Cursillo that we hadn't seen in years, and when she saw Carolyn, she hugged and hugged her. The love we felt during and after Carolyn's sickness was phenomenal."

The family drew closer than ever before, Carolyn said. "Before, all were caught up in their own lives and almost never together at the same time." But after she came home, "there was almost no room at the dinner table."

"A lot of the things we used to take for granted we don't take for granted anymore," Johnny said.

"This made me realize that things do happen in life. This isn't a trial run. This is the real thing.

"Our faith in Jesus has to be real, too."

(This story is an update of one that appeared in *The Florida Catholic* in September 1989. The original report was written by Dave Finnerty.)

TWENTY

She Fell Four Stories Into the Arms of Jesus

+≒═≒+

Her friends had just left. Now she hung from her balcony railing four stories above the street. She let go and began to fall....

Elizabetta Maroni (not her real name) had an Italian father and a Spanish mother. Her parents were divorced and she lived with her mother in Spain. At fourteen years of age, however, she became very rebellious and went to Rome to live with her father. He began to abuse her sexually and, even though he had a series of lovers, he had an ongoing sexual relationship with his daughter.

He provided Elizabetta with all her material needs and sent her to psychiatrists. At one point, she told the psychiatrist, "I think my father is the devil." The doctor said, "That's because he is acting like the devil."

Naturally, Elizabetta was not well adjusted. She couldn't break free of her father and she had periods of severe depression during which she was heavily sedated.

Elizabetta was suicidal, although her doctors didn't think she was serious about killing herself. Her friends, however, kept a close watch on her until that night when they left her alone and she decided to end her life by jumping off the fourth-floor balcony.

Below, in Via Monserrato, Enrico, a seminarian, heard her falling body and just barely escaped being seriously hurt or killed. He stooped to her. Her head was bent backward and she wasn't breathing. He gently brought her head forward, and she began to breathe. She opened her eyes.

Enrico asked, "Are you a Christian?" She said, "Yes." He said, "Are you sorry for all the sins you committed in your life?" She said, "Yes." Jumping the gun quite a bit, Enrico said, "Then I absolve you of all your sins."

The ambulance arrived very quickly and the medics put her on a stretcher, loaded her into the ambulance and left for the hospital.

Enrico tried several times to see her in the hospital but she was so critically ill they would not allow him. He left for summer vacation and when he returned, Elizabetta was no longer in the hospital. He thought she surely had died. She had two broken arms, two broken legs and other serious injuries.

Two years later, a man from the United States, Scott Williams, was in Rome. One evening, at Mass, a woman came in, attracted by the singing. She sat next to Scott and later, they struck up a conversation.

He told her he was studying theology. She asked why and he

said, "I want to get to know God better." She said she did, also. The woman was, of course, Elizabetta.

She told Scott that she had tried to kill herself two years before. She now believed in God and she had two reasons for believing in him.

"First," she told Scott, "I am alive. I'm walking fine. Second, I am really at peace and very happy. I talk to God all the time."

Over the next couple of weeks, she told Scott the story of her unhappy childhood and the fourteen years of sexual abuse by her father.

And she revealed to Scott just how determined she had been to kill herself. After her friends left that night two years before, she had walked onto the balcony and attempted to climb up on the railing. She felt a hand push her back, twice, and she now believes it was God.

But she was so determined that she climbed over the rail, hung there and then let herself drop.

She told Scott that since she woke up in the hospital, she has felt the presence of God in her life. But, Scott discovered, Elizabetta had never really gone to church in her entire life. She didn't understand who Jesus was or anything about his redemptive death.

Scott began to tell her about Jesus and "she was full of questions." Most of all, she couldn't understand suffering and she was puzzled why Jesus had to suffer. He explained the cross to her.

During that time, Scott, a layman, was living with some

monks. One of the monks was the seminarian, Enrico. He asked Scott, "Who was that girl I saw you with? Is she American?"

"No," Scott responded, "she's Italian."

"Where does she live? Via Monserrato?"

"Yes," Scott responded.

"Was she the girl that jumped?"

"Yes."

"I was there," Enrico said. "I heard the sound of her falling through the air."

Scott introduced Elizabetta to Enrico. She had no recollection of his ministry to her that fateful evening. Enrico continued contact with Elizabetta and introduced her into Neo-Catechumenate, a lay movement that helps people learn more about their faith and grow closer to God.

Elizabetta said that while she was in the hospital, doctors discovered she had bipolar manic depression and changed her medication. She is on lithium, and the medicine is really helping her.

She would like to be healed completely, to be rid of depression once and for all, and she and her friends pray for that.

But, today, Elizabetta Maroni is a happy, peaceful and good Christian.

She could never have guessed, when she let go of that railing, that instead of falling to her death, she was going to fall in love with Jesus.

TWENTY-ONE

Faith, Prayer and Doctors Made Her "Cancer Free"!

✛━━✠

Therese M. Celmer had been married five years and had two children, Patty and Jack, when she discovered she had cancer. It was June 1989.

Therese's husband, John, is a computer specialist with the federal government. Therese has a busy life as a stay-at-home mom. She is active in their parish, St. John Neumann in Gaithersburg, Maryland, as a lector, in the adult education program and in the intercessory prayer network.

Her story has appeared in New Covenant magazine (February, 1999) and in a booklet she wrote, "Restored to Health – A Personal Testimony of Healing."

In speaking with Therese, you become aware of two things. One, she conveys a certain serenity and a deep *faith; two, she discusses her healing as matter-of-factly as a farmer might discuss the blessing of much needed rain. No high energy hype here, just a positive and unwavering conviction that God healed her through prayer and medicine.*

My journey began one day in mid-June 1989. I looked at the wooden steps leading down to the concrete floor and experienced a fear that my youngest child who had just begun to walk might fall down those stairs and be injured. I surrendered both of my children, Patty and Jack, to the Lord at that moment: "I give them to you." Only, in God's all-knowing way, the Lord was actually taking *my* life.

A mole removed from my left thigh that same week was diagnosed as a malignant melanoma, the deadliest of skin cancers. I knew as soon as I received the diagnosis from the doctor that my life was securely in God's hands. I had surrendered my life to God the day I put my children in his hands.

In July, I underwent the first of five surgeries for my melanoma, spanning the years from 1989 to 1995. I also began a regimen of frequent doctor visits and medical tests to monitor my condition.

In November of 1991, I discovered a protrusion in my groin on the same side as my original melanoma. The next month, another one appeared. John perceived what these developments suggested and encouraged me to go see my oncologist. The doctor scheduled a biopsy for just after the Christmas holidays.

During Advent that year, I was powerfully affected by the accounts of the Nativity in the Bible. I read of Mary receiving the news that she would be the mother of the Redeemer and how she trusted God to work things out so Joseph would understand. I reflected on my own situation. I, too, faced difficult circumstances. I did not know what the future held any more than Mary had. She said, "I am the Lord's servant. May it be to me as you have said" (Lk 1:38). I thought God was asking me to consent to his will in my life. I chose to say yes to God.

Going into the operation in January 1992 to remove two enlarged lymph nodes, I felt the peace of God. The pathology report indicated that the melanoma had spread to the regional lymph nodes. Three weeks later, I had a lymph dissection, at which time additional lymph nodes were removed.

Discussion with the doctors after my recuperation centered on whether I should try an experimental therapy. There was no standard treatment for melanoma beyond surgical management and close observation. John spent a considerable number of hours reading medical literature to learn of new developments in melanoma research. John and I talked over our findings with my doctor.

My doctor said that my immune system had successfully fought the melanoma for two and a half years and that fact was an encouraging indicator of the strength of my body's immune system. There was no evidence of more cancer in my body, he said, and I could opt to wait and see what medical progress would be made in cancer research in the next couple of years.

I felt strongly that I wanted to be active in my children's lives. I knew I was the heart of the family, that I meant everything to my husband and that my presence in the home was vital. The Lord taught me a priceless lesson at that time. With my medical situation uncertain, I could not afford to find myself, in five to ten years, fighting melanoma and facing the teenage years unprepared. The Lord made me aware that I must train them in lifelong character traits.

I wanted my children to live godly lives. God gave me the grace to teach them spiritual principles. I often reviewed for them what was important in my life, and I shared my faith with them. I shared with them the order of my priorities: having a personal relationship with God, the importance of family time, the development of skills—and plenty of fun. Thursday night became game night in our family.

Over the next three years I learned a lot about accepting myself. I recognized ways in which I discovered or at least acknowledged my worth. I had to give up some grandiose ideas and plans for what makes a successful Christian family but in doing so, I began to experience an inner freedom as I let go of fear, pride and justification by works.

The Lord gave me a tremendous inner healing as he helped me realize that my health really mattered to him. I became aware that I could not be the servant of the Lord that I wanted to be as long as I did not care for my physical well-being. I realized that I had not been getting sufficient rest.

As I embraced the pruning of the Lord, my life became more integrated—-spirituality, practical considerations and relationships blended together and there was more contentment in my life which was a blessing for the entire family.

All along, people prayed for me and with me, especially before major medical tests. One day, as I was being anointed by a priest, I sensed that I was a temple of the Holy Spirit. The presence of God's life in me put all evil, such as sickness, in subjection to Christ. The power of the Cross had defeated the power of death. Even in suffering cancer, I knew the victory of Jesus' death and resurrection.

Then, another setback. On May 30, 1995, a routine physical exam noted a Mass in the left breast. I thought it was a cyst. I did not connect this with melanoma, as I had believed that metastasis would be internal, most likely involving the organs. By July, the breast Mass increased in size and a nodule appeared in the upper armpit area of my left arm.

Both growths were excised and biopsied in August. Both tumors were metastatic melanoma. I was now Stage IV, a medical term often used when cancer spreads beyond the primary site to a distant location in the body.

We were concerned since few patients with Stage IV metastatic melanoma survive beyond two years. Facing a life-threatening battle with cancer, I knew that the Lord had my life in his hands. I trusted in him; however, it was a very stressful time. I prayed for a miracle.

One day in prayer, I sensed that Mary, the mother of Jesus, prayed for me. I sensed that she prayed that the melanoma would never go to the organs. I was absolutely surprised to have received such an impression in prayer as I did not have a particular devotion to Mary. Afterward, I read in my Bible the account of Jesus and Mary at the wedding feast in Cana (see Jn 2:1-11). There, Mary requested that Jesus respond to a need the people had on that occasion. Jesus performed his first miracle and demonstrated his glory to his disciples.

In the autumn of that same year, CAT scans showed two additional sites: a second Mass in the left breast and an enlarged

---

The Power of Mary's Intercession

(At a wedding in Cana, the hosts ran out of wine. Mary, the mother of Jesus noticed this.) ... Jesus' mother told him, "They have no more wine." Jesus replied, "Woman, how does this concern of yours involve me? My hour has not yet come." His mother instructed those waiting on table, "Do whatever he tells you." As prescribed for Jewish ceremonial washings, there were at hand six stone water jars, each one holding fifteen to twenty-five gallons. "Fill those jars with water," Jesus ordered, at which they filled them to the brim. "Now," he said, "draw some out and take it to the waiter in charge." They did as he instructed them. The waiter in charge tasted the water made wine, without knowing where it had come from; only the waiters knew, since they had drawn the water. Then the waiter in charge called the groom over and remarked to him: "People usually serve the choice wine first; then when the guests have been drinking awhile, a lesser vintage. What you have done is keep the choice wine until now." Jesus performed this first of his signs at Cana in Galilee. Thus did he reveal his glory, and his disciples believed in him (Jn 2:1-11).

lymph in the chest. Doctors recommended a systemic treatment. They said the best options for me were only available in
medical research settings. For three years, I had been reluctant
to pursue any experimental treatment. Now I had to decide
whether it was a direction to take.

One day I read Sirach 38 and the Lord impressed upon me
the honor that should be rendered toward the medical profes-
sion. I saw that the Lord wanted to integrate natural healing
with conventional medicine in the pursuit of health. Both are
gifts he has given us. I was not to regard medical research neg-
atively. After praying for guidance and in consultation with
doctors, with John's full support, I made my decision to seek a
systemic treatment for my condition.

In November 1995, I learned of a research project experi-
menting with a melanoma vaccine at the National Institutes of
Health, the premier United States government-funded
research hospital, located near my home in Maryland. There
were rigorous standards for acceptance into clinical studies and
several medical tests were required to evaluate my eligibility.

I saw the hand of God at work in my being accepted into
that particular clinical study. For example: the federal regula-
tory agency approved the vaccine only two weeks before I
entered the clinical study; laboratory tests determined that my
blood specifications were appropriate for the study; a biopsy of
some of my cells revealed that the cells expressed a genetic code
that was being targeted by this very vaccine. Again and again,
I saw that I was in the right place at the right time.

John's sister suggested that our entire family pray for my

healing at the National Shrine Grotto of Lourdes in Emmitsburg, Maryland. John's great-uncle was the chaplain and director of the Grotto, and he celebrated a healing Mass in the chapel for me in early December 1995. Thirty relatives joined me in seeking God's healing grace. I was very touched by the outpouring of love shown me on that day. In addition, I received the Sacrament of the Anointing of the Sick before I began my treatment at the National Institutes of Health.

From December 1995 through May 1996, I participated in a clinical trial at the National Institutes of Health that used the experimental melanoma vaccine. I received four injections, one every four weeks from mid-December to mid-March.

In between vaccinations, I underwent several research procedures as an outpatient. Many were grueling on my body. However, I experienced the consolation of the Lord's great love for me. I learned that the Lord runs to those who are suffering. I sensed that there is a powerful exchange between God and the sick, even if the person is unfamiliar with him as a personal God who loves him or her.

I was able to commute to the clinical center, and this meant I could spend time with my family and the children did not have to spend a lot of time away from home. It helped me, too, knowing there were birthday celebrations to plan and school projects that needed my assistance. Our family led a normal life, but my heart ached as I watched my children experience the common anxieties of having an ill parent.

Going into the clinical trial, I was aware of two things. First, I believed that God wanted to demonstrate his glory by healing me. Second, I had a strong conviction that God wanted to honor the work of my doctors. I expected that God wanted to bless them. I thought perhaps the Lord wanted to touch the team of doctors and nurses by offering them an opportunity to participate in a healing. I prayed for blessings for the doctors and nurses.

Sent To Do What Jesus Did ...

(Jesus summoned his twelve disciples and sent them out on a mission.) ... As you go, make this announcement: "The reign of God is at hand!" Cure the sick, raise the dead, heal the leprous, expel demons. The gift you have received, give as a gift (Mt 10:7-8).

In February, I returned to the National Institutes of Health for the first evaluation scheduled for eight weeks after I had begun the treatment. I had thus received two of the four injections of the melanoma vaccine. The test results showed evidence that my tumors were shrinking. The doctors, my family and I received this news with great joy and appreciation.

I began to believe and observe in myself that I was being healed. In early April, I could feel that the breast Mass had disappeared. Measurements made from CAT scans demonstrated that the lymph node in the chest was continuing to decrease in size. My health was improving dramatically.

I was filled with gratitude and realized that the Lord was healing me for a spiritual purpose. The gospel exhibits the great desire Jesus has to heal. He sent his disciples out to heal (see

Mt 10:7-8). The Lord promised that signs, such as healing, would accompany the gospel.

I understand now that healing is integrally joined to the message of salvation. Healing shines light on the resurrection of the dead. Christ's work of salvation is not complete in us until the redemption of the body on the last day, when Christ returns in glory. Divine healing bridges the gap, in the earthly sphere of time, in Jesus' own resurrection and our resurrection on the last day. Therefore, healings are significant signs of the coming of Jesus, the fullness of salvation, the resurrection of the body and the glorious kingdom of God.

I realized that God wanted me healed in the context of medical intervention, not through a miracle independent of medical care. Besides leading to a deeper sanctification in me, I was sure that he wanted to bless the physicians and nurses involved in my care. I wanted to cooperate with his plan to show them his love—and the Holy Spirit showed me a way to do so and still respect their privacy.

I asked a rabbi in 1996 about the possibility of having the names of my doctors and nurses included in their prayers during Passover. He agreed. I also requested that a priest I knew offer a Mass of appreciation and healing on April 30. I experienced great joy in celebrating the liturgy of thanksgiving for all God was doing in these people's lives. I again received the Sacrament of Anointing at the end of Mass and received prayer for healing.

Ten days later, I had another series of tests and exams after which I was told that the cancer was completely gone. It was noted in my medical records that I was free of disease.

I have remained cancer-free ever since May 1996 and have been declared a "complete responder" to the vaccine. And I have become a symbol of hope to many in the field of medical research.

In March 1997, I was asked by the National Cancer Institute to present my medical history before the Commerce Subcommittee on Health and Environment of the U.S. House of Representatives. One significant fact about my medical case that I shared at that time was that I received no additional therapeutic treatment before, during or since the administration of the vaccine.

It is my understanding that God used the experimental vaccine to heal me. I will honestly say that to anyone who asks and is interested in my case. I know that God was glorified. I am happy to bear this witness to society with full confidence that I am giving the glory to God. I am forever grateful to him for healing me.

TWENTY-TWO

He Was Healed of Lou Gehrig's Disease

+>==—=<+

During the summer of 1992, Don Jeager was diagnosed with Amyotrophic Lateral Sclerosis (ALS), Lou Gehrig's disease. ALS is always fatal but, as Don tells it, "Thanks be to God the Father, his Son, Jesus Christ and the Holy Spirit, I no longer have the disease."

Don is an Episcopalian. When he received the diagnosis from two specialists, he sought help in the church. Fr. David Wilson, rector of All Saints Episcopal Church in Winter Park, Florida, and Canon Jim Glennon, author of several books on healing, joined lay leaders in the church in laying hands on him and praying for healing. "My first ever 'religious experience' occurred when I felt a warmth and peace, leading me to be convinced that I would be cured," Don said. "I was even ready to dispose of the ankle and foot brace I was wearing."

Don studied Canon Glennon's books, *How Can I Find Healing?* and *Your Healing is Within You.* He received Communion, holding in mind the image of Christ's blood washing over the damaged parts of his spine and nerves, healing the diseased parts. He used *The Life Application Bible* in prayer and study and attended healing services each week at All Saints. Physical therapy sessions attempted to slow the inexorable decline of his body.

Don believed he was cured and experienced spiritual tranquility and hope. "God blessed me with divine peace such as I never experienced before and certainly never under such life or death stress. Because of the extreme nature of my problem, I got out of God's way and let him work his will in my life. It's a shame that it took something of this magnitude to teach me a lesson I've been trying to learn for years."

Don continued to seek qualified medical advice. He made an appointment with a doctor who was a professor of neurology at a well-known university. "While I was waiting at the professor's office with my wife, God gave me an irrefutable sign that even someone as dense as I could recognize. My skin temperature rose dramatically and an encompassing peace came over my body. My wife noticed it and confirmed it. I told her the tests would be perfunctory and we'd be out of there.

"The professor kept telling me to be patient during the exam and appeared to confirm through physical inspection that I was cured. However, he ran an EMG (a nerve response test) that confirmed a diagnosis of ALS. But I told my wife I was cured and time would prove it."

He continued his prayer and study and asked God for a sign that the "mustard seed" was growing. He got his sign during a physical therapy session a month after his visit with the professor. "The exercise people asked me to lift some weights with only my lower legs. They wanted to establish a baseline for further exercises. With my lower leg weakened through muscle atrophy due to the disease but with absolutely no strain, grimacing or hanging on to the handles, I lifted the maximum machine weight of 220 pounds. The word flew all over the center. God had further revealed his cure to me."

Continuing good health management, Don made an appointment at the Cleveland Clinic, one of the few and best hospitals in the United States specializing in ALS. En route, he attended a convention where he visited more than thirty companies his company represents. He shared the story of his illness and his belief that God had healed him. "But," he said, "to comfort unbelievers, I assured them that I had organized my company to survive my death.

"Once in Cleveland, the doctors extended my stay to two days, including three hours of EMG tests by two different doctors. The chief physician said that the medical personnel in Florida 'might not believe me, but I see over 150 ALS patients a year and you neither have nor show signs of ever having had ALS.' 'Praise God,'" Don exclaimed and he threw away his brace and went snow skiing.

"I'm now in the post-healing stage, sharing with people. I used to work about sixty hours a week, including many weekends, but I cut back on my hours. I spend more time listening to God. I'm sure he has something special he wants me to do. As a reminder of my illness, I still have a weakness and pain in my left leg and right hand, the first extremities to be attacked by the disease."

As in many cases of miraculous healing, Don said that "the devil attacked me and tried to intrude on my blessed experience. He did so mainly by attempting to instill fear that the healing wouldn't last or I didn't deserve it." But Canon Glennon's books, especially *How Can I Find Healing?*, deal with fear and through God's help, Don no longer has that fear. As he joyfully proclaims, "I don't fear fear!"

In November of 1995, Don was in for another test of faith. He had a heart condition that deteriorated and he had to have open heart surgery. "The lesson for me is that we'll be tried on many occasions, but we must maintain our faith that Christ will comfort and heal us. I am now well. Praise God!"

TWENTY-THREE

The Healing Led to the Canonization of Edith Stein

This story, by Rebecca Drake, editor of The Catholic Observer *in Springfield, Massachusetts, first appeared in* Our Sunday Visitor *(May 11, 1997). It is presented here, with minor editing, through the gracious permission of the author.*

Twelve-year-old Teresia Benedicta McCarthy of Brockton, Massachusetts, is a seventh-grade student who likes to swim and play the piano.

She has no memory of the day in 1987 when, at the age of two, she swallowed sixteen times the lethal dose of Tylenol.

In April of 1997, Pope John Paul II officially attributed the girl's miraculous recovery from irreparable liver damage to the intercession of then Blessed Teresia Benedicta of the Cross, a

Carmelite nun who died at Auschwitz.

Papal recognition of a miracle attributed to the intercession of a potential saint is generally the last stage before canonization.

Born Edith Stein, Saint Benedicta was a Jewish native of Wroclaw, Poland (then part of Germany), who converted to Catholicism at the age of thirty-one. She devoted her life and teaching to the cause of peace and to the reconciliation of Christians and Jews.

As Hitler's influence expanded, Jews in Germany first faced harassment, then increasing danger. In 1938, Stein and her sister fled to the Netherlands to take refuge in a Carmelite cloister, where the Nazis permitted them to stay.

But after the Dutch Bishop's conference issued a letter opposing Nazi persecution, Stein and her sister were deported to Auschwitz along with other Catholics of Jewish descent who had found temporary haven in the Netherlands. Stein died in the gas chamber on August 9, 1942.

Stein was beatified on May 1, 1987, less than two months after the cure of Teresia Benedicta McCarthy, the daughter of Melkite Father Emmanuel Charles McCarthy and his wife, Mary.

Father McCarthy, now rector of St. Gregory the Theologian Melkite Byzantine Seminary in Newton, Massachusettes, tells of his daughter's miraculous cure. "She remembers nothing of it. Life has just gone on," he said. His daughter had been named after the woman believed to have saved her life.

He recalled how the little girl was diagnosed as terminal just days before she walked out of Massachusetts General Hospital "with a balloon in her hand and no medical prescriptions."

Father McCarthy, a priest of the eastern rite of the Catholic Church, was ordained in Damascus, Syria on August 9, 1981. In 1984, he was reading about Stein and noticed that the date of her execution was August 9.

Further research turned up two more significant events that occurred on this date: the bombing of Nagasaki in 1945, and the execution of Franz Jaegerstaetter, an Austrian Catholic who refused to kill for the German military, at Brandenburg Prison in Berlin in 1943.

And at 8:15 P.M. on August 8, 1984, just as the date August 9 dawned in Auschwitz, Teresia Benedicta McCarthy was born in Massachusetts. Benedicta was the twelfth and youngest child in the McCarthy family.

"Edith Stein was just a name in my mind until I recognized the date," Father McCarthy said. As he learned more about the details of Stein's life, "her story became more and more important in my life.

"On Passion Sunday 1938, Edith Stein formally made an offer to God of her life for peace in the world," he continued. "I've often thought that Edith Stein's offering her life to God, that was what was intimately tied to this event [Benedicta's cure]."

Two days after Benedicta was born, Father McCarthy concelebrated a Mass for the Edith Stein Guild at St. Patrick's Cathedral in New York City.

When he told Guild members about his newborn daughter

named after the Carmelite nun, the child was given a lifetime membership in the Guild and a special cross, combined with the star of David, that is worn by life members of the Guild.

Years before the question of a miracle arose, Father McCarthy noted the uniqueness of Stein's vision. "When you read [about] her life, you would be hard-pressed not to sense the deep mystery in it. It's in the atmosphere of the holy somehow," he said.

But Father McCarthy and his wife were not thinking about miracles when they came home the evening of March 20, 1987. They were greeted by two of the older children with news that every parent dreads: Benedicta was in the hospital, in serious condition from an overdose of Tylenol.

As Benedicta was rushed to a major hospital in Boston, the McCarthys began a four-day ordeal of pain and prayer.

By March 22, the child's liver had swollen to five times the normal size and, after she developed an infection, doctors told the distraught parents there was nothing they could do for her.

While doctors waited for approval of a liver transplant, the McCarthys prayed. "The whole family said a rosary for Benedicta," recalled Father McCarthy. "It was out of our hands completely."

At the suggestion of Mary McCarthy and her sister, Teresia, they also decided to pray to Edith Stein. While Father McCarthy conducted a retreat in North Dakota, his wife called several dozen friends and relatives, asking all to pray to the martyred nun for Benedicta's recovery. The "star cross" was placed on Benedicta's hospital bed.

By the time Father McCarthy returned from North Dakota the night of March 24, the child's liver had begun to function again and she was off the critical list. Though doctors had said there was definite kidney damage, Benedicta's liver and kidneys were functioning normally when she left the hospital less than a week later.

"It definitely, definitely was a miracle," said Mary McCarthy. "We're so thankful every day for her. It was amazing. From the time she came home from the hospital, she was running around outside like a [normal] two-year-old."

Still, the McCarthys did not attempt to publicize the story of their daughter's remarkable recovery until a reporter for *The Church World*, the diocesan newspaper of Portland, Maine, heard Father McCarthy mention Benedicta's healing.

When the reporter approached the priest and asked for an interview, Father McCarthy initially declined. It was his wife who insisted that the story be published, the priest recalled. "Mary thought it ought to be known," he said, noting that his wife had never sought the public limelight.

The story appeared in *The Church World* in May 1987 and was later reprinted in the October 1988 issue of *Catholic Digest*. After that, the McCarthys began to get phone calls from people all across the country who were interested in Edith Stein. The story of the potential miracle then became the subject of an investigation by the Archdiocese of Boston.

Carmelite Father Kieran Kavanaugh was living at the community's monastery in Brighton, Massachusetts, when the investigation into the miracle began nearly ten years ago.

Because of his proximity to the place where the healing took place, he "accidentally" became vice-postulator for the cause of Edith Stein's canonization.

Asked to summarize the investigation process, he said, "You need really two miracles. First the miracle, then a miracle to get the miracle approved."

Once the investigation is initiated by the bishop of the diocese, Father Kavanaugh explained, a tribunal is convened to examine the information about the cure and the prayers said to a specific saint.

Sworn testimony is taken from doctors, nurses and others who have firsthand knowledge of the event. The person who was cured must also be examined by two doctors.

After overseeing the diocesan investigation, the vice-postulator then sends the sealed report to the Vatican, where the proposed miracle is investigated by both medical and theological panels. "There were ups and downs over the years," Father Kavanaugh said of the process.

The canonization of Edith Stein marks the culmination of a fifty-seven-year journey for Passionist Father Victor Donovan, a member of the Edith Stein Guild for forty years.

Father Donovan has developed a friendship with Stein's niece, Suzanne Batzdorff, and has devoted his life to the reconciliation of Jews and Christians.

"I am so delighted about the evolution of Edith Stein's story and about this miracle, which took place in my own backyard," said Father Donovan, a native of Randolph, Massachusetts, next door to Brockton. "The miracle of Edith Stein has taken place all over the world. She is God's way of telling Christians and Jews to pay attention."

Meanwhile, for Father McCarthy, the message of Edith Stein's life and the miracle of his daughter's cure point to the profound mystery of God's promise of salvation for all people.

"She teaches us how we should be relating to Jewish people," said Father McCarthy. "We should be standing beside them, dying with them." He said that the saint reconciled the Jewish-Christian separation "in her own person. She never lost that identity."

And even as the family rejoices in the miracle of one child's life, they remember another child who died on April 4, 1986. "Just as that child should not have died," Father McCarthy said, "Benedicta should not have lived."

Reflecting on the experience of the last decade, of a child lost and another saved, Father McCarthy concluded, "The ultimate effect of it has been a deepening of the sense of the mystery of the ways of God. In the end, God is beyond words."

TWENTY-FOUR

Nancy, a Victim of Hate Mail

We'll call her Nancy and her husband, Tom. Circumstances make it advisable that they remain anonymous.

Nancy is one of those beautiful people who seem to be everywhere someone is needed. Wife, mother, working woman, active parishioner, Nancy has a gentle spirit, a quick smile, a ready word to encourage, compliment and empathize.

It's hard to believe that such a woman would be targeted for vicious lies, for stalking by anonymous letter. But that was what happened.

Out of the blue, Nancy began to get unsigned hate notes, filled with vile accusations. The notes were always left on her desk, but no one ever saw who left them. However, Nancy, her supervisor and her husband, Tom, are fairly certain who is attacking her in this way. It can't be proved and the person has never been caught.

Remember What Jesus Said....

Blest are you when they insult you and persecute you and utter every kind of slander against you because of me. Be glad and rejoice, for your reward is great in heaven; they persecuted the prophets before you in the very same way (Mt 5:11-12).

The attacks unnerved Nancy. It was bad enough when the letters were left on her desk but then the stalker threatened to send them to her parish priests. Both her pastor and associate pastor received letters maligning Nancy. She was beside herself with grief. "Now," she thought in her confusion, "my priests will believe all those lies."

Of course, they didn't. They knew and respected Nancy and Tom and assured her that they understood the letters were lies. Her associate pastor, a veteran of fifty years in the priestly ministry, spent an hour with Nancy, but at the end of the session, she was still crying in anguish over the unjust attacks. He gave her a big hug and said, "let me carry that burden for you." Nancy felt relief rush over her. The understanding of her priests reassured her but she realized she had another problem. Even though she and Tom prayed for Nancy's enemy, she had begun to hate the person causing her so much pain.

It happened that Nancy was scheduled to serve as a lector in a special service in the church that evening. Little did she know she was on the verge of a miracle—a spiritual healing.

As she got up to do the reading, she felt spent and couldn't imagine how she would get through it. The church was dark except for the light on her stand and a light over the sheet music at the organ. The church was very quiet.

"I got a chill that shook my entire body," she said later, "and I just knew I wouldn't be able to do the reading. The organist coughed to let me know he was ready to begin. He was going to play background music while I read from Scripture. I got another chill and began to read.

> ### The Power of Forgiveness
>
> (Jesus said:) "When you stand to pray, forgive anyone against whom you have a grievance so that your heavenly Father may in turn forgive you your faults" (Mk 11:25).
>
> "Forgive us our trespasses as we forgive those who trespass against us ..." (From the Lord's Prayer).

"Suddenly, it was as though there was no one in the church but God and me. I felt his presence. I read the passage and returned to my seat and started to cry. I realized that I no longer hated that person. God had taken the hatred from my heart and I was at peace. My tears were now tears of joy."

Nancy now speaks of the situation with a certain calmness. She still feels the pain of being so hated by someone. She knows, too, that her "enemy" is someone she forgives and for whom she prays.

A spiritual healing, turning hatred into love. Quite a miracle in anybody's book!

TWENTY-FIVE

A Priest Alcoholic Tells His Story

＋══════＋

In his own words, an elderly priest tells his story of faith, despair and rediscovered faith. This is a healing story in which prayer, the support of friends and the Twelve Step Program of Alcoholics Anonymous (AA) came together to restore a priest to his priesthood.

I'm a Catholic priest, originally from the Midwest.

I'm an alcoholic. I didn't come from an immediate family of drinkers. My mother and father abhorred drinking because alcoholism was on both sides of their family. They were dead set against it.

I didn't start drinking until I was nearly forty years old. It was on the night that John F. Kennedy was elected president. I was with a bishop and four other priests in this rectory in a big parish of about five thousand families. We had about twenty thousand people in our parish.

The bishop said, "Since we have our first Catholic president, I think we ought to heist one." I was the only one there who didn't drink, so I had some ginger ale. I said to one of the priests, "Well, on this momentous, happy occasion, how about if you spike my drink with some Cutty Sark?" And you know, I was off and running then.

I loved the taste of that stuff right away. In retrospect, I can say I became an alcoholic at that very moment. From then on, I was always anticipating a drink and I didn't want the day to go by unless I had a drink. One drink led to another. I don't think I ever had just one drink in my life. I was like the alcoholic in the story who went into a bar and told the barkeep, "Set me up six individual shots of whiskey." The bartender looked at him and asked, "Are you sure you know what you're doing?" He answered, "Yes, six!"

The bartender set six shot glasses before the alcoholic, who began drinking the second shot, then the third, fourth, fifth and sixth. The bartender asked, "Why didn't you drink the first one?" The man answered, "Well, it's the first one that gets me drunk."

So I never had one drink. That's because I'm an alcoholic and an alcoholic cannot stop with one drink. If I take that first drink, I'm off to the races. And I proved it, over and over and over again.

It took me sixteen years and a lot of agony and not much ecstasy to get straightened out, to get relief from this disease. I didn't want to be an alcoholic, but it was on both sides of my family. An alcoholic can often trace his disease through his family tree. I certainly could do that.

It got so bad, I began to drink alone. I began to let down on my conscience, my morals, my priesthood. I functioned well. I probably could have done much better had I not been drinking. Maybe I couldn't have. Maybe I had to go through that to get where I am today.

But it got so bad that after twenty-four years in the priesthood and being a pastor and having so many good ministries, my addiction got so bad I walked away from it all. "Lord," I said, "I am not worthy to be your priest." I was beginning to be a disgrace to myself, to my family, to my Church, to my vocation, to my parish. I walked away and went into hiding for about six months.

Finally, my brother caught up with me when I asked for help. He said, "You know, there are two things about you. You can't handle alcohol. I think you're an alcoholic. Second, you can't tell the truth. I don't mean cash register truth, I mean truth to yourself. You're a psychological liar to yourself."

Then he said, "Are you willing to get help?" I said, "Yes, I am." He said, "Are you willing to go to AA?" I said I was. Now I might have told a lie there, because I was willing to do anything to get out of trouble. I don't know whether I was willing to do anything to get away from alcohol.

I did go and for three years I stayed dry. Then I went into a monastery for a year and a half. It is only by the grace of God and the benignity of my family and my bishop that I was able to go way out west to a diocese where a bishop, a friend of my brother, was willing to give me an opportunity. I took that opportunity and got back "on the job" as a priest. After a year, I was incardinated—formally received—into that diocese as a priest. You know how I celebrated that? By having a drink.

I sort of fooled the bishop for awhile. He made me a pastor. But on Christmas Eve, imagine this for a priest, I was carried out of the rectory, drunk.

I was put into this celebrated treatment center for priests and religious, and I stayed there for six months. Then I got out. I don't know whether I learned anything or not, but I'll tell you I nearly went out of my mind while I was there. I was paranoid, withdrawn. I felt that people were making fun of me. Maybe they were.

It got so bad that one time, in a small group setting, I began to crawl around on all fours like a dog, and they just let me do it. And I knew I was doing it and I couldn't help myself. Finally some person began crying and picked me up, hugged me and took me back to my room.

I remember around St. Patrick's Day, I was rooming with this other priest who was trying to get straightened out, and I was freezing to death. I had on two sweat suits but I couldn't get warm. I was sweating and had chills. I was in bed and I thought I was going to die. I started the countdown, saying Jesus' seven last words from the cross. When it came to "It is finished," I screamed and shouted, "I'm gonna die! I'm gonna die!" And the priest said, "My God, can't you say any prayer? Can't you say the Memorare?" I said, "I know it but I can't say it," and he said it. And a calm came over me then and I began to feel warm and began to feel as though I was coming back to myself.

I got back on the job after that. I had seven good years of ministry as a pastor on a college campus. But I got away from going to AA meetings and being honest with myself. And right

> ## The Memorare
>
> Remember, most gracious Virgin Mary, that never was it known that anyone who fled to your protection, implored your help, or sought your intercession, was left unaided. Inspired with this confidence, I fly to you O Virgin of virgins, my Mother. To you I come. Before you I stand, sinful and sorrowful. O Mother of the Word Incarnate, despise not my petitions, but in your mercy hear and answer me.

before I again took that "first drink," after seven years, I drove around for two weeks with a bottle of Cutty Sark in the trunk of my car. Then I took that drink. I can almost taste it as I tell the story now. I was in my kitchen, living alone, and I took an Old Fashioned glass, no ice, and filled it up with scotch. "I'll have only one drink," I said. That's how devious we are when we're drinking. I drank that, and said, "Well, that was so good, I'll have another."

Finally, I had to surrender again. I was sent to a treatment center for priests and religious for three months. They weren't into reduction therapy the way the other place was, where they had almost stripped me of all my humanity. They were coming at it from the other direction, trying to build up my ego, dignity and self-esteem. I didn't hurt so much at that one, and I appreciated what they were trying to do.

I came out of there, and I was made an associate for a couple of years. I couldn't make it. Finally, I was picked up in a hotel by a couple who searched until they found me. They took me into their home, and eventually I got in touch with the bishop.

I went off to another monastery around early December. I spent Christmas in the monastery and then was shipped out to another place for six months. The object was not only to get me sober and maybe get me in touch with myself, but to tell me in no uncertain terms that I could never be a practicing priest again.

I remember going in for my evaluation about a month after I arrived at this center. Everyone on the faculty of that institution was trying to tell me that I was worthless, I was no good and I could never be a priest again. And when they had all finished—and I hadn't known that termination of my priestly ministry was part of the reason I was there—the head of the flaying session told me what a skunk I was, what a disgrace I was to everybody. He asked me what I had to say for myself.

I looked at the group. "I heard what you said, I understand what you said, but I have to tell you that I don't agree with what you said. You said I could never be a priest again. I think I can. I believe that I can. And by the grace of God, I hope I can."

When I said that, the leader of this flaying ceremony cursed me and said, "Who the hell do you think you are? You midget-mind, going against this distinguished faculty with all their degrees. You who have disgraced the Church are trying to tell these people that they are wrong?" And he went on in that vein. At the end, when he quieted down, I said, "With all due respect, I repeat what I said. I believe I can be a practicing priest again. I will hope and pray for it."

Needless to say, I was devastated. The rest of the time at that center was devoted to reducing me, telling me that I would have to work at McDonald's or some such place. My counselor said that so often, I couldn't stand hearing it. But she did say something significant to me: "I want to tell you, priest, the only thing you have left in life is God and AA."

A month before my six months were up, something quite providential happened. I received a letter from the chancellor of my diocese telling me a certain person and her husband were trying to get in touch with me. They were demanding that they be put in touch with me. He said it was up to me whether I wanted to respond to them. He gave me their address and phone number.

At first I didn't recognize the name, but then I recognized the woman's first name. Her last name was her married name and thirty years before, I had helped her get into a Carmelite convent. I hadn't heard from her since.

I called her on the telephone. I said, "Why do you want to get in touch with me after thirty years?" She said, "God told me to." When I had interviewed her about going into the convent, she had told me she was having some colloquies with Jesus—and I was the only one who had believed her. She said to me, "Now, it's time for payback." She had gotten sick and left the convent and had later married.

I told her, "I'm in trouble." She said, "I know you are and we want to help you if we can. You helped me to get in; I'll help you to get out."

They offered me a room in their home. When I left the center, I was allowed to say something. At Mass—I was not allowed to say Mass—we had read John's Gospel about Peter's response to Jesus' three questions, "Peter, do you love me?" I was reminded that Jesus told Peter that as a young man he went where he wanted to go but that when he was old, they would take him where he would not want to go. I said, "That's the way I feel now. St. Peter didn't want to go in that direction, but he did it and that's what I'll do. I turn myself over to God."

I left. I traveled about a thousand miles to my destination, to the room the couple were providing for me. I rang the doorbell, and there was this former Carmelite nun. She invited me in, and she and her husband showed me the room. In the room there were four cats. I hated cats.

I was not allowed to wear clerical attire, be a public priest or say public Mass. I could say private Masses, all by my lonesome. But I had a congregation. I had the four cats. They even listened to my homilies, and fell asleep, too.

The day I arrived, I asked where the parish church was. I went there the next day at 8:30 A.M. The first thing I did after

Mass was to identify myself to the pastor, whom I had never met. I said to him, "Would you be my spiritual director?" He said, "I will be your friend."

This wise priest did not take me in hook, line and sinker. He measured me. He said he would be praying for me. Eventually, he let me work there. I told him that they had said I could never be a priest again but that I wanted to stay close because I was living on faith, hope and love. He let me do some Scripture courses and some convert work and train the altar servers. I was anonymous there, and some people began to figure out that I was a priest, but I never said anything about it. Eventually the pastor brought me to the table at the rectory on the Monday nights when the priests had their family meal together.

Meanwhile, I was going back to the treatment center every six months. That was over a period of two years, for continued rehabilitation and to be sure everything was OK.

The pastor got me out of the "cat house" and saw to it that I had a studio apartment. So I kept going to daily Mass and attended all church ceremonies and devotions and participated in parish life. I didn't work, but the priests were helping me and I was getting a minimum stipend, about $700, from my diocese. I was able to survive.

I had a sponsor in my Twelve Step Program in AA. He helped me out, too. He walked the walk and talked the talk with me every day.

The Twelve Steps

The Twelve Steps of Alcoholics Anonymous have been adopted by many other spiritual movements. The priest sharing his story here has used these simple, progressive steps in spiritual direction and in spiritual growth programs. Basically, the twelve steps are as follows:

1. A person admits he or she is powerless over addiction to alcohol, sex or drugs, or powerless over some other destructive and harmful behavior pattern.

2. The person believes that God, who is greater than he or she is, can restore a person to health and sanity.

3. A person makes a decision to turn his or her will and life over to God.

4. The next step is a thorough and honest, even fearless, examination of one's life.

5. One admits to God, oneself and one person the exact nature of his or her wrongdoings and difficulties.

6. One is ready and willing to have God remove all defects of character.

7. Then he or she asks God to remove those defects.

8. Next, he or she writes down the names of the people one has hurt and is willing to make amends.

9. One makes amends, directly, unless to do so would injure that person or others.

10. Continue to examine one's life and to admit when one is wrong.

11. Pray and actively seek a closer relationship with God as one knows and understands God.

12. Having been spiritually awakened and healed, one tries to bring this message to others.

I think the best prayer I ever said in my entire life was the first time I went to the AA community to which I now belong, before I got to know the priests and people of this wonderful parish. I was scared to death. My family was instructed to abandon me, which they did. I had no friends, knew nobody in the area.

Outside that meeting room, the first time I went there, I said to God, "God, you're the only one I have. Please help me. Lead me to somebody who will take me by the hand and show me how to get this program so that, at least, if I can't be a priest, I can be a super human being." I think that is the first time I really took the first step—to realize I am helpless and need God—completely, thoroughly, meaningfully. And I've realized it ever since, thanks be to God.

After about two weeks in that AA community, I found my sponsor. He was a guy who was suffering from terminal cancer of the colon and the throat. But he spoke sense at the meetings. He spoke convincingly. I knew he was a Catholic because he attended the same daily Masses I attended.

I remembered something the late Bishop Sheen had said during a priests' retreat. He said that in seeking a spiritual director, look for someone who is suffering and accepting it without groaning about it and someone who is trying to get close to God. There was that combination in this layman.

When I first asked him to be my sponsor, he said, emphatically, "No!" So, I grabbed him and in "purple language" I said, "Listen, you! I'm a Catholic priest, you've got to help me!" And, responding in language even more purple, he put his finger in my face and said, "If I help you, you'll do exactly what I tell you or you're done!"

I did what he told me. He went to three meetings a day with me for a year. He took me to the movies, fed me. And he got completely back into the Church, coming to all church events. He had had a recovery experience himself, when he cried out for help, and after thirty-five years he had come back to the Church. And now he's refining it. He has a special devotion to the Blessed Mother. Every Monday, we both made the novena to Our Lady of the Miraculous Medal for my restoration to the priesthood. One day he said, "You'll be back in ministry on the feast of the Immaculate Conception next December." And on December 8, I was restored to the priesthood.

I had written to my former bishop, who had said I could never be a priest again. I asked him to end my suspension and permit me to be a retired priest so I could function publicly as a priest and earn my keep.

He responded that so long as he was my bishop he would never give me that privilege. He said that "if some bishop is crazy enough to give you a chance, maybe I'll let you go if he'll take you completely." A bishop would have to accept me as one of his own priests in his diocese, and all ties with my former diocese would be severed.

The bishop of the diocese in which I was now living, with the help of a retired bishop, got together and saw to it that I was incardinated into this new diocese. That took effect on December 7. On December 8, the feast of the Immaculate Conception, I celebrated my first public Mass in my restored priesthood.

As my hero, Bishop Sheen would say, "Restored friendship is sweeter than unbroken love."

Since then, these are the happiest days of my priesthood and my life. Praise be to you, Lord Jesus Christ!

AFTERWORD

Do miracles still happen? Does God still heal people when they ask him to heal? Is it really "Catholic" to believe that God heals people even if they don't go to Lourdes, Fatima or some other approved site of apparitions? What does the Church have to say about the healing power of prayer?

In 1998, Archbishop John Clement Favalora of Miami, Florida, wrote about healing in his regular column in his archdiocesan paper, *The Florida Catholic*. Noting that 1998 was the "Year of the Holy Spirit" in the three-year preparation for Jubilee 2000, Archbishop Favalora discussed the presence and power of the Holy Spirit in the lives of ordinary people.

The archbishop surely does not see the Spirit working only in the charismatic renewal, but he wrote specifically about this movement since, he said, it is through it that "a new Pentecost has come, not only because of the institutional renewal that resulted from the Second Vatican Council, but because of the widespread personal renewal that has come about through the charismatic renewal."

He said that the renewal is Catholic and that it began in 1967 when a group of Duquesne University students and teachers were "searching for a richer meaning in their lives and a deeper relationship with the Lord." On a retreat, "they prayed that the Holy Spirit would come into their lives ... and indeed, something happened during those days of prayer and fasting which the students had never before experienced. They felt a sense of liberation, an inward release of something that had been there all along—a release of the special work of the Holy Spirit within each individual ... they began to pray with much more fervor (and) more importantly, the fervor overflowed into every aspect of their daily lives."

From these small beginnings, the Catholic charismatic renewal has grown "to encompass more than 15 million people in the United States and 72 million worldwide."

In his columns, the Archbishop discussed various aspects of the renewal in the Holy Spirit that has swept through the Church as well as various gifts of the Spirit, including healing.

A Synopsis of Archbishop Favalora's Treatment of Healing

The Holy Spirit is known as the Healer, the Unifier, the One who makes whole that which is broken. In our technological age, many people wonder: Do miraculous physical healings take place today, or was that power limited to Jesus and the Apostles? An adage of the Church holds that "as you pray, so do you believe." So if we pray for healing, we must believe that it is possible.

- Medical science is now discovering that people of deep faith, and those who have other people praying for them, heal more quickly than others. This is true even when they don't know that other people are praying for them.

• There are many different kinds of healing: emotional and spiritual healing such as that which takes place when a husband and wife reconcile or brothers and sisters cease feuding or families are healed of damage due to alcoholism, drugs or violence. When these ills are cured, we believe the Holy Spirit has been manifest in a special way in the lives of these people, directly or indirectly, knowingly or unknowingly.

There are people who have the gift of healing such as Sister Briege McKenna, O.S.C., who was herself healed as a young nun of crippling arthritis. Today she has a worldwide healing ministry and conducts retreats for priests. On a retreat for priests in Rome, she told a story of a priest who felt lukewarm about his priesthood and who had decided to leave his vocation after twenty-five years. She asked him when was the last time he had made a good confession. He told her it had been twenty-five years. She told him to go to a fellow priest and make a good confession. Years later, she found out that he had remained a priest. That confession had made all the difference in his life.

His healing was no less miraculous because it was spiritual rather than physical. The insight that enabled Sister Briege to ask that one question, and the force that moved the wavering priest to visit her, are proof that the Holy Spirit is still working and manifesting himself in the world.

Not every prayer leads to the desired healing. We must bow to God's wisdom and providence—his plan for our lives when healing does not take place immediately or the way we envisioned. But if indeed we believe the Church is continuing the mission of Jesus on earth, then we must believe that healings of all sorts can take place, just as they did in Jesus' time, through the power of the Holy Spirit.

It is precisely through the working of the Holy Spirit within us, in union with the Father and the Son, that our broken world will be healed. That is the mission of the Church, to help bring about that healing, that wholeness, so that the world may reflect the union of love of the Trinity itself. When that is accomplished, we believe, we will have heaven on earth.

All of us must work toward that goal, and we must allow the Spirit, whose work is sanctification and wholeness, to take us there. The Catholic charismatic renewal can help make that happen.

It is not the only way, of course. Many people who have allowed the Holy Spirit to take over their lives are not part of the movement. But judging from its "good fruits" during the past thirty years, the charismatic renewal is a significant way for many people to discover and release the power of the Holy Spirit in their lives.